"FACE DOWN"

"FACE DOWN"

Barbara Golder

Indianapolis

2009

Contents

MY DEEPEST APPRECIATION

- To my Lord and Savior Jesus Christ for bestowing on me revelation and enabling me to birth what He has seeded in my belly.
- To my loving husband Bishop Donald L. Golder, for his unwavering support. Next to the Lord, you are my most cherished friend.
- To my five beautiful children, Iren, Devon (Shenita), Jerimaine, and Briah, and my six grandchildren, Lil Iren, Devion, Donavan, Lil Devon, Amaya and Dallas, who are my pride and joy. Thanks for keeping me grounded and humble.
- To my adorable mother, Mrs. Bernice K. Scott for introducing me to the love of my life "Jesus Christ" and for being the ideal example of a virtuous woman. Thanks for always loving and supporting me.
- In memory of my wonderful father Mr. Nathaniel Scott, a mighty man of valor. I love and miss you so much!

Introduction

The most significant or prominent surface of an object is the face. The face is the surface that is presented to view and thus it represents the entire object. For example, when you look at the face of a clock, you decide whether or not you want to buy the clock based on the way the face looks. Rarely do you have the retailer open the interior of the clock so that you can view its inner contents. The same is true when people select mates. Usually there is an immediate attraction to the facial area that draws attention to the other person. After the initial attraction, then relationships are formed and people are able to determine whether or not they are compatible.

One of the greatest acts of disrespect that a person can give is to slap someone or to spit in someone's face. People take great pride in the way they present their faces. Cosmetic companies and plastic surgeons are making millions of dollars selling products and performing surgeries that will enhance the appearance of people's faces.

As I fleeced the Lord about the title of this book, He began to reveal to me the significance of bowing, face down, in prayer. In Eastern countries bowing ones face down toward the ground is the usual posture of worship or reverence. When Easterners pray they sink to their knees and hands, and then place their faces on the ground. This form of prayer and worship is done both publically and privately. When an individual bows "face down" or lays prostrate in prayer, he or she assumes "humility," a virtue that many lack today. Even in scripture we see reference to "face-down" prayer:

> 3 And when all the children of Israel saw how
> the fire came down, and the glory of the LORD

upon the house, **they bowed themselves with
their faces to the ground upon the pavement**,
and worshipped, and praised the LORD,
saying, For he is good; for his mercy endureth
for ever.
2 Chronicles 7:3

"And thus are the secrets of his heart made
manifest; and so **falling down on his face** he
will worship God, and report that God is in you
of a truth."
1Corinthians 14:25

"And the people believed: and when they heard
that the LORD had visited the children of Israel,
and that he had looked upon their affliction,
then **they bowed their heads** and worshipped."
Exodus 4:31

There are many different types of prayers. The
Jewish people have a prayer book called a Siddur, which
contains a set order of daily prayers. These prayers
include: morning prayers, night prayers before retiring for
rest, prayers for the feast of Purim, prayers for Sabbath,
prayers for meals, etc. Although all prayer is
commendable and necessary for spiritual growth, you
don't need a book of prayers in order to begin
communicating with God. The Lord wants a relationship
with you. He wants His children to humble themselves
and pray! God is not concerned with your diction; He is
not interested in how many big words you know, He's not
interested in your grammar, He just wants us to talk to
Him. Consider the following scriptures:

5 "And when thou prayest, thou shalt not be as
the hypocrites are: for they love to pray
standing in the synagogues and in the corners

> of the streets, that they may be seen of men.
> Verily I say unto you, They have their reward.
> 6 But thou, when thou prayest, enter into thy
> closet, and when thou hast shut thy door, pray
> to thy Father which is in secret; and thy Father
> which seeth in secret shall reward thee openly.
> 7 But when ye pray, use not vain repetitions, as
> the heathen do: for they think that they shall be
> heard for their much speaking.
> 8 Be not ye therefore like unto them: for your
> Father knoweth what things ye have need of,
> before ye ask him.
> Matthew 6:5-8

Build a strong relationship with your Heavenly Father through "Face Down" prayer. Allow God to usher you into new dimensions in Him! The following is a simple prayer guideline given to us by our Lord Jesus Christ:

> 9 After this manner therefore pray ye: Our
> Father which art in heaven, Hallowed be thy
> name.
> 10 Thy kingdom come. Thy will be done in
> earth, as it is in heaven.
> 11 Give us this day our daily bread.
> 12 And forgive us our debts, as we forgive our
> debtors.
> 13 And lead us not into temptation, but deliver
> us from evil: For thine is the kingdom, and the
> power, and the glory, for ever. Amen.
> Matthew 6:9-13

Just as there are various types of verbal prayers, there are many different physical positions one can assume to pray. Praying while standing with your hands lifted up often represents praise, thanksgiving and celebrative prayer. Other positions of prayer include sitting, kneeling, walking, lying flat, etc. Prayer can be done anywhere an individual is able to remove their mind from their current surroundings and concentrate on Jesus Christ.

The focus of this book, however, is the importance of assuming a position of humility when approaching the Father. We must understand where our worship and praise come from. Is it simply self-devising, or does it result from our first coming before God in sincere humility? When we bow and lie prostrate we are doing homage to our Savior. As we humble ourselves at His feet "as dead," God is pleased and subsequently He will lift us up!

> 17 "And when I saw him, **I fell at his feet as dead**. And he laid his right hand upon me, saying unto me, Fear not; I am the first and the last:"
> 18 I am he that liveth, and was dead; and, behold, I am alive for evermore, Amen; and have the keys of hell and of death."
> Revelation 1:17-18

Even Satan realized the significance of humbling oneself to authority. Satan asks Jesus to "fall down and do homage to me":

> 4 "Again, the devil taketh him up into an exceeding high mountain, and sheweth him all the kingdoms of the world, and the glory of them;
> 9 And saith unto him, All these things will I give thee, **if thou wilt fall down** and worship me."
> Matthew 4:8-9

Satan did not want adoration and praise from Jesus! No, He wanted Jesus to humble Himself and place Himself below Satan! Satan's deepest desire is to be "like the Most High." Satan wants to be exalted and the only way that could happen would be if Jesus prostrated Himself before Satan! When we lower our bodies, our hearts and our spirits and pray "face down," we give God the honor He is due and we make the devil madder than a junk yard dog!

The American Heritage Dictionary defines "face down" as the following: "To attain mastery over or overcome by confronting in a resolute, determined manner: face down an opponent in a debate; faced the enemy down; to confront boldly and courageously. To contend with physically, fight, assail, attack, battle, brawl, clash, combat, confront, cross swords, vie with, face, feud, row, spar, duel, and counterattack."

When we "face down" in prayer, not only are we humbling ourselves and giving God honor, we are positioned for war against the devil!! In the earth realm the most common ground attack position is standing with fists in front of your face and legs slightly apart to brace your body. But in the spirit realm, the most powerful attack position is "Face Down!"

> 17 "Ye shall not need to fight in this battle: set
> yourselves, stand ye still, and see the salvation
> of the LORD with you, O Judah and Jerusalem:
> fear not, nor be dismayed; to morrow go out
> against them: for the LORD will be with you.
> 18 And Jehoshaphat bowed his head with his
> face to the ground: and all Judah and the
> inhabitants of Jerusalem fell before the LORD,
> worshipping the LORD."
> 2Chronicles 20:17-18

You see, Jehoshaphat, Judah and all the inhabitants of Jerusalem knew the secret to their success was "face down." Prayer is the key, and faith unlocks the door! God's protection and all of His richest blessings are available to each of us if we will "face down" and pray! As you read this book I challenge you to face down the enemy, face down strongholds, face down sickness, face down poverty, face down immorality, face down defeat, face down generational curses, face down everything that is coming against your purposed destiny in Christ Jesus!

Chapter One

Prayer Is Basic

Throughout the history of mankind, prayer has been practiced and recognized as a vital tool that links the natural realm to the spiritual realm. The dictionary (The American Heritage Dictionary n.d.) defines prayer as the following: "An act of communion with God, such as in devotion, confession, praise, or thanksgiving: A fervent request: The slightest chance or hope." Even those who don't believe in the one true and living God, the Lord Jesus Christ, believe in the effectiveness of prayer.

Muslims study the Quran, and are required to pray to Allah several times each day. A requisite to each Muslim is to pray the "Salaah" five times per day at respective times, facing in the direction of Mecca. They are also required to recite the "Fatiha" which can be prayed up to seventeen times each day.

Through the teachings of **Hinduism**, its followers are taught the importance of prayer. They don't advocate the worship of one God; as a matter of fact they pray to thousands of different deities. Hindus believe that each one of their gods reigns supreme over different areas of life and they pray to each god in their respective area of authority. For example, prayers are offered to the deity Shani Dev in order to ward off evil and remove obstacles from one's life.

Buddhism teaches their followers not to petition a god, but to pray to a higher awakening in order to achieve Nirvana (the state of joy and supreme happiness). Buddhists believe that through regular meditation one can actually clear his mind and become one with the universe.

Even **Satan worshipers** pray! The following story written March 15, 1998, by Reverend Bruce Goettsche, sent chills down my spine:

> "Jay Kessler the former President of Youth for Christ and the current President of Taylor University, was on one of his frequent flights. When lunch was served the young man next to him declined a lunch tray. During the whole lunchtime this man sat with his head bowed, apparently in prayer. Kessler was impressed (and maybe a little humbled) by the man's devotion. He commented to the young man that he wondered if he was a Christian because it appeared that he was fasting. The young man replied with words that shook Kessler to the core of his being,
> "I am a Satan worshiper and the members of my church have agreed to fast every Friday at noon. During that time we pray that the leaders of the Christian world will fall. We pray that they will fall into sexual sin, and that their family life would crumble."

As I reflect on the countless well-known, high profile Christian leaders that have succumbed to sexual immorality since the inception of this demonic crusade, I am enraged! The public humiliation, the massive attack on the integrity of the church, and the effectiveness of Satan's campaign has grieved my spirit! If there were ever a time that the body of Christ needs to come together and pray, the time is *NOW*! We must stop bickering; complaining and criticizing each other, and bind together (IN PRAYER) as one united force against the devil!

> "**A**nd when he was come near, he beheld the city, and wept over it,

Saying, If thou hadst known, even thou, at least
in this thy day, the things which belong unto
thy peace! but now they are hid from thine
eyes.
 For the days shall come upon thee, that thine
enemies shall cast a trench about thee, and
compass thee round, and keep thee in on every
side,
 And shall lay thee even with the ground, and
thy children within thee; and they shall not
leave in thee one stone upon another; because
thou knewest not the time of thy visitation.
And he went into the temple, and began to
cast out them that sold therein, and them that
bought;
Saying unto them, It is written, My house is the
house of prayer: but ye have made it a den of
thieves."
Luke 19:41-46

Satan has marshaled his forces together and is
launching his final attacks, but very many in the church
are asleep!

"For there are certain men crept in unawares,
who were before of old ordained to this
condemnation, ungodly men, turning the grace
of our God into lasciviousness, and denying the
only Lord God, and our Lord Jesus Christ."
Jude 1:4

Church has become big business! The sanctuary is
not sacred and holy, but rather a place for fashion shows,
fish dinners and entertainment. We are so concerned with
church programming and the big revenues that these
programs bring into the church's bank accounts, that
many churches have forgotten prayer! I was surprised to
see people from other congregations attending Tuesday

prayer meetings at my local church because their churches don't have scheduled prayer gatherings.

A church without prayer is POWERLESS and is just another social club! I believe that the church should meet the needs of the people, but this will only be accomplished through effectual, fervent prayer!

> "…The effectual fervent prayer of a righteous
> man availeth much."
> James 5:16

Satan has neutralized and demoralized much of the church and the only way to regain our authority and position of noble influence is through prayer! Yes, prayer is the solution; however it is often the answer nobody wants to hear.

> " For this cause we also, since the day we heard
> it, do not cease to pray for you, and to desire
> that ye might be filled with the knowledge of
> his will in all wisdom and spiritual
> understanding;
> That ye might walk worthy of the Lord unto all
> pleasing, being fruitful in every good work, and
> increasing in the knowledge of God;
> Strengthened with all might, according to his
> glorious power, unto all patience and
> longsuffering with joyfulness;
> Giving thanks unto the Father, which hath
> made us meet to be partakers of the inheritance
> of the saints in light:
> Who hath delivered us from the power of
> darkness, and hath translated us into the
> kingdom of his dear Son:
> In whom we have redemption through his
> blood,
> even the forgiveness of sins:"
> Col 1:9-14

When problems arise, advice and solutions to these issues are sought from pastors, counselors, and anyone who we feel can offer the support needed. These consultants are expected to sit and listen attentively to the problem and then offer some grand and miraculous solution. Although scripture confirms that confession and counsel is good, the answer to every dilemma is found through prayer.

"Confess your faults one to another,
and pray one for another,
that ye may be healed.
The effectual fervent prayer of a
righteous man availeth much."
James 5:16

If we would just learn to effectually and fervently seek God in prayer, we would find all of the answers to every situation we may encounter.

The devil has deceived the children of God into believing that prayer is simply a casual act of gratitude that we offer up to God on various occasions. We pray when we eat our meals, thanking God for our food and asking Him to purify it and sanctify it for the nourishment of our bodies... we pray when we go to bed at night, asking Him to protect us from hurt, harm and danger as we sleep... Some even get a quick prayer in during the morning, thanking God for another day. Many Christians have learned how to hit the floor, face down, and pray when trouble arises in their lives, but the sad fact is that most people don't have a lifestyle of effectual and fervent prayer.

Many Christians pray short, casual prayers throughout the day. A casual prayer is the kind of prayer that you pray when you are driving or when you're washing the dishes or cleaning the house. Don't get me wrong.... Prayer anytime and in any way is great!

"Men ought always to pray, and not to faint;...
And shall not God avenge his own elect,
which cry day and night unto him...
I tell you that he will avenge them speedily..."
Luke 18:1,7,8

Yes, God hears your prayers whenever you pray, but when you pray casually, you are not totally dedicated to the conversation you are having with God. Your attention is divided. For example, when you're praying and washing the dishes, you've got one ear to God but the other ear is open to hear what the children are doing in the next room... When you are praying and driving the car, you have one ear to God and the other ear on the road. You are very much aware of where you are going and what other cars are doing around you. I've had some really anointed casual prayer while driving, so I am aware of how prayers can shift from casual to something more intense and powerful. When this happens while you are driving, please pull over to a safe place and let God have His way!

Prayer at work is another wonderful place for casual prayer. Prayer at work is generally casual because you are still held accountable to your surroundings. For instances, if you work in a quiet corporate office, it is probably unacceptable for you to indulge in the moaning, groaning, crying and loud outbursts that often accompany prayer.

Although casual prayer refreshes us during the day, there comes a point and time when casual prayer is just not enough. Think about the personal and intimate relationships that you have: Where would they be if you communicated with your love ones only on a casual basis? Think about how you feel when you are talking to someone and he or she is distracted by other things. Although it is possible to communicate in this way, it is definitely not the most effective means of communication.

Husbands, the best way to start an argument with your wife is to continue looking at the football game while she is attempting to communicate with you. Now, women, during a football game is probably not the best time to attempt to have a talk with your spouse, but the point is, when you talk to your spouse, you expect his or her undivided attention.

"For the LORD thy God is a consuming fire,
even a jealous God."
Deuteronomy 4:24

God desires time alone with His children. Prayer should be a part of our spiritual journey that transforms our confusion, pain and suffering into fulfillment, joy and meaning; A time of intimacy with God. **Prayer was never meant to manipulate God!**

In these last days God is looking for people who are willing to commit to a lifestyle of DEDICATED PRAYER. A Christian magazine quoted a survey showing that the average Christian spends about three (3) minutes each day in prayer. What was even more alarming was that the same survey showed that Christian leaders (preachers, teachers, etc.) spend an average of seven (7) minutes each day in prayer.

Although these statistics are unfortunate, the fact is that many churches have gotten caught up in the business of "having church"; they have become more concerned with church programming then they are about the church's foundation. Having assisted my husband in ministry for the past six years I have fallen victim to the BUSINESS OF CHURCH. When my husband heard the voice of the Lord commission him to the position of Pastor, I jumped in with both feet. My desire was to not only support my husband, but to obey God. I thought having a Master's Degree in Business would enable me to assist my husband in building the "Church" on sound business principles.

We began attending church and leadership conferences, taking classes and trying to find the most effective marketing strategies on which to build our church. We learned everything from the best form of advertisement and promotions, to the ideal color that a tithe envelope should be.

While I firmly believe that a church should employ sound business tactics, I have found that the best marketing strategy for any church, business, family, community or nation is A DEDICATED PRAYER LIFE! Programs are great, but they are like the windows and doors to ministry. Prayer is the foundation – if there is no hard core prayer, there is no firm foundation and the ministry, business, family, community, and nation cannot stand. You see, the foundation is the basis on which a thing stands or is supported – it is the infrastructure if you will...

> "Therefore thus saith the Lord GOD, Behold,
> I lay in Zion for a foundation a stone,
> a tried stone, a precious corner stone,
> a sure foundation..."
> Isaiah 28:16

Jesus Christ is the sure foundation that God has laid in Zion. Anyone who builds their trust, hope and dreams on this foundation, will never fall! But in order to build on Jesus, you must first have a relationship with Him!

Prior to my husband's accepting the call to pastor, life was good. Yes, we had our occasional struggles, but trouble took on an entire new meaning after we became totally committed to Kingdom building.

> "Yea, and all that will live godly in Christ Jesus
> shall suffer persecution.."
> 2Timothy 3:12

Yes, the moment that you decide to live a life that is holy and set apart from the world, you will suffer persecution. The old spiritual says,

"Sure I must fight, if I would reign,
Increase my courage, Lord;
I'll bare the cross, endure the pain,
Supported by Thy Word."

Although we will all suffer, there is an entirely different level of persecution in store for those individuals who submit to the call to the pastoral office. I realize that, to many, the offices of Pastor and First Lady look very glamorous, and you may feel as though you desire the position. My words of caution to you are twofold: First, "Don't Believe the Hype" and second, "Make Sure God Has Called you." I would need to write another book in order to tell about all of the trouble that my husband and I and our family were hit with when we embarked upon this awesome journey; but I will say that we went from driving a new Escalade and a new Lexus to driving an old rusted van that smelled like mildew, the windows were broken, and the keys would not come out of the ignition.

Not only were our finances attacked, but our children were attacked also. One son was incarcerated on multiple counts of drug possession and dealing and sentenced to 10 years in the state penitentiary. The specifics surrounding his struggle are detailed in forthcoming chapters. Another one of my sons was shot at multiple times and forced to leave the state due to a hit that was placed on his life. Terrible threats were being made by one of the city's notorious drug dealers and for a while our entire family was in grave danger. The following is an excerpt from a poem written by my oldest son as a tribute to his father. This literary composition vividly depicts the chaos which infiltrated our lives:

"......I apologize for the lies and the pain that I
put you through.
The constant disruptions in school and my
criminal minded attitude...
I know it gave you the blues.

Or when the police kicked down your front
door,
put guns to your face and made you kiss your
own floor.
Ransacked your home putting they hands in
your underwear drawer...
Looking for me!!!

And I know that it hurt you that I didn't follow
the steps of your foot...
studying the King James Version and learning
the depth of the Book.
But I was intrigued by the hustlers and
gangsters and increased finances,
the cars, jewels, and women that it attracted at
first glances...
it made me foolish.

But you never turned your back on me, you
always lent your support...
you let God be my judge and the world be my
court.
You stuck your chest out in front of me like a
soldier protecting his fort,
or a father protecting his son... you became fire
like a torch!!!

You tried to make it clear to me,
why you worshiped a God you couldn't touch
or see.
You would break it down to try to ease my

confusion,
between what I can see and hear, or my school
which taught me evolution.

My delusion would cause me to study the ways
of the Quran,
Kabala, Torah, never Satanist, but Atheist,
Agnostic, Vice Lord & Islam.
But by you not only preaching, but living a life
that exemplifies Christ,
caused me to realize that He is The WAY, The
TRUTH and The LIGHT!

Now beyond a shadow of a doubt I believe and
I know His Word is true,
cause not only can I feel His presence, I can see
the very face of God when I look at you."
Iren Donald Golder

The effects of the enemy's crusade to destroy marriages and families through sexual immorality, hit our home as well. Satan launched a vicious assault on our marriage. One of the members of our church (who had a sexual affair with my husband 24 years prior) decided to make an appointment with me and maliciously disclose the intimate, nasty details surrounding their encounters. She was careful to cite the dates, places and times of each occurrence and she presented names implicating other people for their involvement.

I'm telling you the devil will set you up! Don't ever think you are getting by. As the old cliché says, "What's done in the dark, will come out in the light!" The devil may hold your stuff for 24 years, but eventually dirty little secrets will be exposed!!!

The enemy was mad, so she turned up the heat and began to divulge the sequel of immoral erotic behavior with countless church members within our church. Our church members and members of other congregations and denominations began calling our home stating that she had come to their churches and shared the report as well. This time there was a new twist on the encounter... people were led to believe that the indiscretions happened recently.

Although this series of sexually immoral events happened long before we began to pastor a church, the knowledge of my husband's infidelity hit me like a ton of bricks! I had been "Gut Punched"! I had no idea that my soul mate of twenty-nine years had broken our marriage covenant on multiple occasions. I will never be able to convey the level of betrayal, hurt, resentment and anger that I felt. Thank God for the wondrous healing POWER of His Blood!

> "Who his own self bare our sins in his own body
> on the tree, that we, being dead to sins, should live
> unto righteousness: by whose stripes ye were healed."
> 1Peter 2:24

Every evil stripe the devil inflicted on me actually conferred strength and wisdom. Anger, bitterness, vindictiveness, self- pity, even divorce were all in the devil's plan for my life; but God said, "Stay, Forgive, Show Compassion, Learn, Grow, Cling to your husband and Do The Work of an Evangelist!"

Through (face-down) prayer, God healed me and enabled me to break free from anger and humiliation. Yes, "...in all these things we are more than conquerors..."! My marriage has healed and God's grace and love is taking us to unimagined levels in Him!

> "And we know that all things work together for good to them that love God, to them who are

the called according to his purpose…..
Who shall separate us from the love of Christ?
shall tribulation, or distress, or persecution, or
famine, or nakedness, or peril, or sword?
As it is written, For thy sake we are killed all
the
day long; we are accounted as sheep for the
slaughter.
 Nay, in all these things we are more than
conquerors through him that loved us.
 For I am persuaded, that neither death, nor life,
nor angels, nor principalities, nor powers,
nor things present, nor things to come,
Nor height, nor depth, nor any other creature,
shall be able to separate us from the love of
God,
which is in Christ Jesus our Lord."
Romans 8:28, 35-39

Although the tribulation, distress, and persecution
that I experienced caused me tremendous heartache, my
suffering enabled me to fully understand what David
meant when he said,

"Deep calleth unto deep at the noise of thy
waterspouts: all thy waves and thy billows are
gone over me."
(Psalms 42:7)

I don't want to make light of my situation. There
was a point in my life that I really didn't know if I was
going to make it! I felt as though I was going to lose my
mind! It was as though one evil was inviting another evil
to come and have a party in my life. The waves and
billows were crashing over me so fast and hard until at
times it was literally hard to breath! I felt as though I was
about to drown!

My pain was not alleviated overnight! My complete deliverance took months of fasting and deep prayer which extended far down below the surface. "Now I lay me down to sleep, I pray the Lord my soul to keep..." was not the type of prayer that could have sustained me during this tragic period of my life.

One writer said that there is a threefold depth which the saints and servants of God are subject to here in this life:

1. The depth of temptation.
2. The depth of desertion.
3. The depth of affliction and human calamities. (T. Horton.)

Within our first 7 years of ministry I can honestly say that we were hit hard with all three! We learned early on that if we were going to see our purposed destiny manifested, we were going to have to go deep!

"And he shall be like a tree
planted by the rivers of water,
that bringeth forth his fruit in his season;
his leaf also shall not wither;
and whatsoever he doeth shall prosper."
Psalms 1:3

If you would allow me to paraphrase this scripture:

"And he (the man or woman who stays in
God's presence through a dedicated lifestyle of
prayer) shall be like a tree planted by the rivers
of water (will be tapped into the source of life
and possess power) that bringeth forth his fruit
in his season (will perform the work that God
has purposed within the appointed times and
places) and his leaf also shall not wither (will
not fail) and whatsoever he doeth shall prosper
(the constant flow of God's mercy, grace, & love

will enable you to flourish…YOU WILL
SUCCEED!)

As a teacher by profession, I have taught many
adults on various levels. As a National Executive Director
and Trainer for a nutrition supplement company, I
traveled to various parts of the country instructing
distributors on how to successfully manage and grow their
businesses. I have taught courses at local Colleges and
Universities and I have taught countless Bible classes and
Sunday school classes. The teaching profession has given
me the opportunity to interact with adults of all ages,
genders and social and economic levels. Although each
person is different and unique, I found some things to be
the same with most people that I encountered. When I
asked my students what they believed they were placed
on this earth to do, most of them didn't have a clue.

At one point in my life, I was clueless also… *I*
wanted to know my purpose, *I* was eager to get on with it
– *I* thought if *I* only knew what the Lord had purposed for
me to do, then *I* could begin doing it. If God would just
show me, then *I* could get a game plan together. *I* could
set some short- and long-term goals and then *I* would
make sure *I* accomplished my purpose!

Does this sound crazy to anyone but me? I
mentioned God once in this phrase… All God has to do is
to show me, **then, I will take over**. All God has to do is
get me started – and **I** will take it from there and make
God proud of me! When will we learn that "**I**" must take
the back seat and **God** must be at the helm of our lives!

"For in him we live, and move,
and have our being…"
Acts 17:28

You will never know your purpose until you really
get acquainted with the source (God) through a life of
dedicated prayer.

Why are so many of God's people walking in defeat – because they haven't tapped into the source. Yes, I was saved (I had the Holy Ghost, evidenced by speaking in other tongues)... Yes, I loved God... Yes, I was living a righteous life... Yes, I paid my tithes... Yes, I read my Bible and Yes, I even prayed... but there was still something missing... I knew within my spirit, that there was more!

> "Having a form of godliness,
> but denying the power thereof:
> from such turn away."
> 2Timothy 3:5

We have become so engrossed with tradition, legalism, and religion, that we neglect plugging into the power source (the Holy Ghost) on a regular basis. It is much easier for men to observe the forms of religion than it is to submit their hearts under the controlling and sanctifying power of the Holy Ghost.

Pastor Dave Roberson says, **"The devil has removed tongues from three-quarters of the church. It's much easier for believers to be deceived by the ever-changing doctrines of man when they have been separated from the primary teaching tools that enables them to learn from the Holy Spirit Himself.** (*Walk of the Spirit The Walk of Power* Roberson n.d.)

> "But ye shall receive power, after that the Holy
> Ghost is come upon you..."
> Acts 1:8

The devil has deceived many into believing that the Holy Ghost is not necessary, and he has convinced some of those who are Spirit-filled that speaking in tongues is a onetime experience. Some holiness churches teach that when you are born again, you receive the Holy Ghost and the evidence of this rebirth is speaking in an unknown language. Once you have spoken in tongues, you really don't have to speak in tongues ever again. Now, if the Lord hits you with a special anointing during a prayer or a powerful service, and you feel His powerful touch, then He (the Holy Spirit) may cause you to begin speaking in tongues again. Although this is true, there is more that is being left out.

A believer can actually start his or her prayer off in tongues (the Holy Ghost) and invoke the presence of the Lord. One can actually kneel to pray and, by one's own will, begin praying in tongues.

"But ye, beloved, building up yourselves
on your most holy faith, praying in the Holy
Ghost."
Jude 1:20

Some believers are greatly stressed and beat-up by the devil because they have not built themselves up on their most holy faith by praying in the Holy Ghost (praying in tongues). Sickness and depression have infiltrated the church as never before. The devil has afflicted the saints with all types of diseases, stress, oppression, depression… you name it, and the church has taken it on.

I've actually heard saints reference their illness as though it were a family member that they don't get along with too much. I've listened to the precious children of God say things like, "My arthritis has really been bothering me today." While some are being delivered, far too many are operating in defeat. Why are they not walking in victory when God said,

"But he was wounded for our transgressions,
he was bruised for our iniquities: the
chastisement of our peace was upon him; and
with his stripes we are healed."
(Isaiah 53:5)

The devil has turned up the heat and he is hitting the church with everything he's got. If we are going to live in victory, we are going to have to commit to more prayer time and crank up our faith! In the book entitled "Think Yourself Well" the author Bernard Ward says the following:

> "The power to heal lies in everyone's subconscious mind and prayer is the one way to create the right mental conditions to release that power. When you pray for healing, you create in your mind the image you want of yourself as a healthy, disease-free person. By remaining faithful to that image, your prayer is answered. Never let yourself admit for a second that you might not be healed, and always end by thanking God for the healing that you know is already at work" (pg 51).
> Dr. Sheri Perl developed a program called "Healing From the Inside Out." (Perl n.d.) In Ward's book, Dr. Perl is quoted as saying, "Healing from the inside out means going inside to the spiritual source of your power, healing first from the psychic, spiritual, feeling-thought plane and then experiencing the change as the energy filters out into the physical layers of your body" (pg 51). (Ward n.d.)

According to Ward, Dr. Perl has had tremendous success in the past 28 years, using this technique to treat seriously and terminally ill patients. The word of God enforces just how powerful the human mind really is:

> "And be not conformed to this world:
> but be ye transformed by the renewing of your mind,
> that ye may prove what is that good,

and acceptable, and perfect, will of God."
(Romans 12:2)

Whether it's healing in your body or another challenge in your life, it's hard to ignore what things appear to be in the natural realm and trust God for the manifestation of what you believe He has already done in the spirit. I'm so glad that God doesn't require watermelon size faith:

> "And Jesus said unto them, Because of your
> unbelief: for verily I say unto you,
> If ye have faith as a grain of mustard seed,
> ye shall say unto this mountain,
> Remove hence to yonder place;
> and it shall remove; and nothing shall be
> impossible unto you."
> Matthew 17:20

Once you decide to believe God for your breakthrough, the devil will do everything he can to attack your senses (what you see, hear, feel, think). The devil will do everything he can to make the evidence in the natural earth realm appear to be the opposite of that for which you believe God.

Twenty-eight years ago I was married to my wonderful husband. We were very young and we couldn't afford a big honeymoon, so after spending our wedding night in a hotel, we went to Saint Louis to see his grandmother who was very ill. While in Saint Louis, I was curling my hair with an electric curling iron. The electric socket was elevated on the bathroom light causing the power cord to hang in front of my face. As I was curling my hair, the curling iron slipped out of my hand and the hot curling rod went directly into my eye. The pain was excruciating! I couldn't even open my eye.

My husband took me immediately to the hospital emergency room. When the doctor looked at my eye there was a large white blister covering my entire pupil. After the examination the doctor informed me that I had damaged my retina so severely that I would not be able to see out of my eye again, and if I did have any sight at all, my vision would be severely impaired.

I was devastated to say the least! All I could think was, *I'm a young newlywed whose blinded in one eye.* The thing that I want to point out here is this: I was saved... I had been saved for many years...

I was raised in church... I had a praying mother and a praying grandmother... but it never entered my mind to pray! I was so absorbed with what was happening to me, I couldn't get beyond the natural realm. I only focused on what the doctor said my fate was; I never once consulted the real physician (God).

As we traveled back home to Indy, feelings of self-pity, depression and disbelief continued to set in. All I could think was, *Why did this happen to me?* A short while after we arrived home, the Lord spoke in my spirit and said, "Ask your husband to lay hands on you and to pray a prayer of healing over your eye."

What you must understand is that it took a great deal of faith for me to even ask my husband to pray for me. Although we had been Christians since we were teenagers, we had never come together to pray or worship God outside of church.

We loved God and we were committed to serving Him (to a certain extent), but prayer wasn't something that we did together. I was actually embarrassed to ask him to pray for me. On one hand I thought, *He's not saved enough to pray for me; I need the Bishop or one of the elders of the church to lay hands on me*; and on the other hand I thought, *He's going to think I'm getting too deep.*

Now that I look back, I recognize that it was the devil filling my mind with foolishness so that my husband and I wouldn't come together in prayer and take authority over the enemy. Eventually, after I couldn't stand the pain any longer, I obeyed God and asked for prayer. My husband looked at me with a small grin, laid his hand on my eye and began to pray a powerful prayer of healing. After he finished, I went to bed and went to sleep.

The pain was still there, but God allowed me to finally drift off to sleep. The next morning when I woke up, the blister that had covered my pupil, was TOTALLY GONE and the pain was too! The moment I stepped out on faith and asked my husband to pray for me, God totally healed me and when I woke the next morning, I saw the manifestation of my miracle!

My father insisted that I go to the eye specialist and have another eye exam. Although I knew that I was healed, I went anyway to satisfy my dad. After the specialist examined my eye, he told me that my eye had 20/20 vision and that regardless of what the doctors in Saint Louis said, my eye was fine. The specialist acted as though I was either lying or the Saint Louis doctors were wrong in their diagnosis. If it had not been for the burn mark on the upper lid of my eye, (which the Lord left in order to prove I was really burned) the specialist would have probably thought I was crazy.

The next day, my mother and I watched miraculously as the burn mark on my upper eyelid vanished. Each hour, the scar got lighter and lighter until it literally vanished completely! After that day, there was no trace of my accident, not one single trace. After all of these years, I have not had one eye problem stemming from the burn. I'm a witness that you can receive a miracle from mustard-seed faith!

Chapter Two

The Gift That Keeps On Giving

The Lord used Prophetess Carolyn Walker, a powerful praying woman, as a catalyst to usher me into another dimension in God. I refer to her as my spiritual mentor because she enlightened me to something so basic, yet so profound. She introduced me to a book entitled, *"The Walk of the Spirit The Walk of Power"* by Pastor Dave Roberson from Tulsa, Oklahoma (Roberson n.d.) Pastor Roberson's book, which explores the vital role of praying in tongues, actually taught me how to pray in the spirit realm. Praying, for me, was a chore. After twenty or thirty minutes of prayer, I had Worshiped God, Praised God, cried out to God, Asked God for forgiveness for all known and hidden sins, prayed for everyone who came to my mind, moaned and groaned.

When I completed my audible prayer, (*my mind in English*) I would be silent to hear the voice of God. I would speak in tongues at various intervals during prayer, but I would always revert to English. I didn't realize what an awesome gift I had in the Holy Ghost nor did I know exactly how to use it. I explain it like this:

Let's say that you were broke and someone gave you a gift of one million dollars. When you received the money in your hand, you instantly became a millionaire. You didn't have to work for the money because it had already been given to you. All you have to do now is to hold on to the gift that was given to you. Being a millionaire will enable you to live a wonderful life of prosperity, free from poverty and the stress associated with wondering how you are going to make ends meet.

But if you take the million dollars and place it in the bank and never use it, then it is impossible to really benefit from it. You may receive some notoriety for having a million dollars and you might be invited to some places to which you otherwise would not have been invited, but just having the name "Millionaire" is not enough.

Now, most of us would not have any difficulty at all spending our million-dollar gift, but just stick with me for a moment; I promise you I'm going somewhere with this illustration. If you never went to the bank and withdrew any of your money, you would still live in poverty and lack. Yes, you would still by all rights be a millionaire... the money was a gift that was given to you, but until you make a withdrawal from the bank, the money will not do you any good. In order to enjoy your money and benefit from it, you must use it!

Well it's the same way with the Holy Ghost. The Holy Ghost is a gift that God gives you and, once you receive the gift that God gives you, you are a Christian. Being a Christian has many benefits, but if you don't use your gift (the Power... the Holy Ghost)... you will not accomplish all of the wonderful and glorious things God has planned for you! You will never know your destiny and your purpose... you will never know exactly what you were released on the earth realm to accomplish. The Holy Ghost is not only your POWER to fight the enemy; it is also your road map to your destiny!

> "Howbeit when he, the Spirit of truth, is come,
> he will guide you into all truth:
> for he shall not speak of himself;
> but whatsoever he shall hear, that shall he
> speak:
> and he will shew you things to come."

John 16:13

When you pray in the Holy Ghost, that's when you will begin to go deep! God will begin to show you things that are forming in the spirit realm. One might say, "Why would I want to know about things in the spirit realm?" Well, there are at least two reasons that you will benefit from knowing what's in store... 1) You can either pray your future blessings into fruition, or 2) you can arrest the enemy's curse before it's able to manifest itself! See, there are things that we as saints go through because we must suffer...

"And he said to them all,
If any man will come after me,
let him deny himself,
and take up his cross daily,
and follow me."
(Luke 9:23)

PAUL FOLLOWS UP BY SAYING:

"For unto you it is given in the behalf of Christ,
not only to believe on him,
but also to suffer for his sake."
(Philippians 1:29)

With suffering comes many needed attributes... strength, wisdom, faith, knowledge, compassion, just to name a few. The prophet Zechariah said,

"...I will bring them through the fire
(suffering),
and will refine them as silver is refined,
and will try them as gold is tried:
they shall call on my name,
and I will hear them: I will say,
It is my people: and they shall say,
The LORD is my God"
Zechariah 13:9

Although the Bible tells us to expect some adversities, there are some struggles that we really don't have to go through. There are situations that we can literally catch and prevent, in the spirit realm, through praying in the Holy Ghost. When you pray in the Spirit, you can actually abort the devil's assignments.

While I was praying in the Holy Ghost, God showed me a vision of a young African girl standing dressed in a lovely, flowered dress. She was a pretty girl with two long pony-tails on either side of her head. She stood still and silent. In the vision I reached my hand out and touched her forehead and prayed for her. The vision was so clear – it was as though I was watching it on a television screen. It was a brief vision that flashed in and out in a matter of moments. After I finished praying, the Lord spoke to my spirit and revealed the message of the vision to me.

The little African girl represented my daughter… she appeared as an African because a foreign spirit was trying to attach itself to her. God instructed me to lay my hand on my daughter's head and pray in the Holy Ghost over her each night and to take authority over that spirit!

You see, that is what a lifestyle of dedicated consistent prayer in the Holy Ghost will do… It will allow you to arrest and cancel the devil's attacks in the spirit realm before they are ever released on the earth realm. While face down in prayer, you must not focus on the enemy and his attacks… Seek God's face…

"But seek ye first the kingdom of God,
and his righteousness;
and all these things shall be added unto you."
Matthew 6:33

So, what are we to seek? The Kingdom of God, which is God… but how do we seek God? Through prayer in the Holy Ghost. And how do we seek His righteousness? By living Holy. The scripture says that if we follow this formula, then all things will be added to us... To what things is Matthew referring?   Great things, little things, heavenly things, earthly things, whatever you desire shall be added unto you.   After Matthew tells us to seek the Kingdom first, he goes on to say,

> "And I will give unto thee the keys
> of the kingdom of heaven:
> and whatsoever thou shalt bind on earth
> shall be bound in heaven:
> and whatsoever thou shalt loose on earth
> shall be loosed in heaven."
> (Matthew 16:19)

Saints, we must learn how to BIND THE DEVIL! Why go through all the hell the devil has planned for you, when you can stop him dead in his tracks in the spirit realm before it ever hits the earth? The point is not to sit around and ponder all of your past heartaches and tribulations, wondering what things you could have prevented. Don't sweat over the past, just seek God's face and allow Him to show you the future.

I was asleep one night and I had a dream of my three sons when they were young children, years ago. My sons are all grown now, (24, 26, and 31) but in the dream they were small... I would imagine about 4, 6, and 11. In the dream my sons had just come inside from playing. I had run their bath water and before we could decide who would get into the tub first, my youngest son jumped into the bathtub fully dressed. I looked at his little, cute face and the dream abruptly ended. I immediately woke up crying frantically.

All I could think about was how sweet and innocent he was. I thought, God... if I could just go back and raise him again... if I could just have another chance to use the Power tool that I have (the Holy Ghost) I am certain that his life would have taken a different direction. You see, my youngest son dropped out of school in his senior year and got involved with drugs. It was obvious that he was not cut out for that type of life because he was constantly getting caught. His friends, who did far worse than he, never got caught, but my son never got away with anything! He ultimately was convicted of dealing drugs and was sentenced to 10 years in prison.

The Lord began to show me that my son would have been dead if he had stayed on the streets. The Lord showed my husband that this son was going to be his heir in the ministry… You see, it's always the ones who give you the most grief who have the greatest anointing on their lives… Why do you think there is so much drama in their lives? It's because the devil is trying to take them out! The enemy wants to destroy them because he knows they have been assigned to tear Satan's kingdom down!

After my youngest son was born, my husband asked God, "Why are we having so many boys?" And God told him, "Because they are going to work with you in Kingdom building." God showed my husband that our youngest child would be his heir in the ministry. I held fast to the old saying, "If God Said It, Then That Settles It!" I believed that all I had to do was to sit back and watch God do His thing. So, while I was sitting back just "Naming and Claiming," the devil launched his attack to abort my son's purposed destiny.

Saints, the Lord will give you precious promises and allow you to know things that He has in store for your future. He may show you things in dreams and visions, he may speak to your spirit in a still, small voice, He may speak to you through a prophet, He may speak to you through scripture, He may even call you by your name… no matter how God speaks to you, when He speaks, you can stand on what He says… for,

"God is not a man, that he should lie;

neither the son of man, that he should repent:
hath he said, and shall he not do it?
or hath he spoken, and shall he not make it
good?
Numbers 23:19

God said, "Yes! If I said it, then that settles it in heaven; now you must settle it on earth! It's already done in the spirit, but you've got to birth it out in prayer!"

"The thief cometh not, but for to steal,
and to kill, and to destroy:
I am come that they might have life,
and that they might have it more abundantly."
John 10:10

The devil not only wants to take away what you already have possessed, he wants to steal your purpose, he wants to destroy your destiny! The enemy wants to steal things out of the spirit realm and prevent you from ever seeing them in the natural. But God has given you POWER to have more abundant life. The American Heritage Dictionary defines Abundance as, "A great or plentiful amount... Fullness to overflowing." So, on the one hand, God has come to give you plentiful overflow, but, on the other hand, the devil has come to steal, kill and destroy your abundance.

I'm so glad that God has placed inside of us everything that we need to overcome the enemy and live victorious lives... for His Word says,

"Ye are of God, little children, and have
overcome them: because greater is he that is in
you,
than he that is in the world."
1 John 4:4

Regardless of how hard the enemy attacks you, remember,

"Nay, in all these things
we are more than conquerors
through him that loved us."
Romans 8:37

Back to my dream... My heart was so heavy that I mourned all day long. When I was in prayer (face down) that evening, the Lord spoke to my spirit and said, "You can't go back and re-raise your son, but I'm going to raise him up better than you ever could!" GLORY TO GOD! Well... I don't remember how long I was face down on the floor that night, but I do know that after hearing God, I was at peace with my son's situation. I wasn't happy that he was in prison, but I knew God would take care of him.

I remember one occasion when the devil tried to steal my peace. I had just finished preaching in Columbus, Indiana, and I was driving home when all of a sudden, out of nowhere, the enemy spoke in my spirit and said, "You are doing all of this preaching and teaching, and you are helping everyone else, but look at your son (in jail). I remember crying like a baby... the tears were coming so fast and so hard that I could barely see the road. I just couldn't shake this feeling of self pity... I felt as though God had forsaken me. I mean I was really having a pity party right in my car.

Somebody once said, "It's all right to have a *Pity Potty* every once in a while, as long as you remember to flush when you finish!" We all go through periods of wondering if God really hears our prayers... Even Jesus Christ felt this agony:

"And at the ninth hour Jesus cried with a loud voice,
saying, Eloi, Eloi, lama sabachthani? which is,
being interpreted, My God, my God, why hast thou forsaken me?"
Mark 15:34

Well, when your faith is shaken, having someone in your life who you know can get a prayer through is a MUST! I immediately called a dear friend of mine who is a co-minister of the gospel and I asked her to pray with me.

> "Again I say unto you, That if two of you shall agree on earth as touching any thing that they shall ask,
> it shall be done for them of my Father which is in heaven."
> Matthew 18:19

While I was still driving, she prayed a powerful prayer and I received victory over the oppression that was trying to silence my ministry. I once again placed my son in God's hand and within forty-eight hours my son was released from jail! You see, I was right on the brink of a break through... The devil knew that my blessing was about to be manifested on the earth realm so he frantically tried to discourage me, and cheat me out of it. God was about to work a miracle, but the devil wanted me to give up.

Instead, I called for help, got a prayer warrior to touch and agree with me and through prayer my son was released seven years before his completed sentence! You can't tell me prayer won't change any situation!

You must understand that when things appear the worst, that is when your breakthrough, your miracle, is the nearest! When we went to my son's court hearing, there were several other cases being heard prior to my son's. The judge that was on the bench was very harsh and merciless. Every case that he heard he denied release. Every time the court room door opened and another prisoner was led in, I could see my son sitting in the holding room with his hands and feet chained. His head was down in his lap and I knew he was discouraged. This was in part due to the fact that the judge who had granted him the hearing was not the judge on the bench, and my son was certain that he was going to end up just like all of the rest of the cases, back in jail.

My son's case was the last case that was heard that morning and when it was time for his case to be presented, the merciless judge got up from the bench, walked out of the courtroom and in walked a man wearing a T-shirt and blue jeans, and drinking a soda. After this man approached the bench, he drapes a black robe across his shoulders, slips his arms in, sat down and called my son into the courtroom.

He quietly reviewed my son's file and then said, "I see all of the accomplishments that you have made while you have been incarcerated; I see you have a supportive family and I am releasing you, effective immediately!

Even after the judge released my son from prison the devil just didn't want to let him go! His paper work had to be processed before he could actually come home. The devil was furious and he tried everything he could to hold things up. First, the papers couldn't be signed by the attending officer because he had left and wouldn't return until the next day. Because of this, my son had to spend another night in jail.

The next day after the paper work had been signed, one of the inmates hung himself in his cell and the entire prison was placed on lock down preventing anyone, even staff, from leaving the facility.

Wow, the devil was really trying his hardest to trip us up, but it was too late... instead of worrying and complaining, we began to pray even more, and, needless to say, my son was released!

Now when I pray, I thank God for bringing forth His promise. Yes... I've learned how to Go DEEP and pray my blessings through! Our single aim and focus must be

God first; and indeed whosoever seeks God first will soon come to seek Him only. You see, I never asked God to release my son from prison within a certain time frame. I gave the situation totally over to God. I trusted that God knew what my son needed better than I did. I held on to the Word of God... Remember, God had already told me that He would raise my son up better than I ever could...

Well, today my son has completed high school, has a college degree from Ball State University, and another College Degree from Full Sail University. God is an AWESOME God and He stands true to His Word!

> "Delight yourself also in the LORD,
> And He shall give you the desires of your
> heart."
> Psalms 37:4

When you find God and consistently enter into His presence, nothing else matters! As you continue praying in the Holy Ghost, you will develop unimaginable faith and trust in God. We must be willing to dig deeper if we are to obtain all of the riches that are available in Christ Jesus. I realize that the nature of humans is to prefer to have every little thing given to us on a silver platter, but that's just not the way God operates. He has already given us everything that we need to take authority... We have dominion!

> "And God said, Let us make man in our image,
> after our likeness: and let them have dominion
> over the fish of the sea, and over the fowl of the
> air, and over the cattle, and over all the earth,
> and over every creeping thing that creepeth
> upon the earth."
> Genesis 1:26

God has already given us supreme control over the earth, but in order to operate in our position of authority, we must fight! God freely gives us the Holy Ghost and the power that comes with it, but we will have to work in order to possess all of the wonderful and glorious benefits associated with His gift.

Think about your children... what type of adults would they become if you never required that they work for anything? We freely and unconditionally give our love to our children, but in order for them to receive an allowance, they must do their chores... in order to have telephone privileges, they must make good grades, in order to go out with their friends, they must adhere to a curfew. Even when our children are rebellious, lazy and disrespectful, we still love them and we still provide for them. We furnish them with food to eat, clothes to wear, a home to live in, etc., but until they line up with the program and work, they will not enjoy all of the privileges that they could otherwise be enjoying. Until they line up with the order of your house and the rules that you have set, they will suffer discipline.

Have you ever wondered why the Lord placed all of the precious stones like silver, gold, diamonds, rubies, crystal, etc. deep within the ground and positioned inside the walls of mountains? Even coal, oil and precious minerals are found nestled within the earth. None of these valuable commodities are easily accessible, thus increasing their value. Mining is a very dangerous and tedious job. Many miners have even lost their lives digging beneath the earth's core, searching for valuable gems.

There is a dimension in God that you will never obtain until you are willing to face down and go deep. Going deep requires great effort. Someone once said, *"Salvation is free, but the anointing will cost you something!"* The question is, are you willing to pay the price?

Are you willing to put your face to the floor and pray all night long? Are you willing to push your plate back and deny your flesh food and water? Are you willing to miss your favorite television show in order to read God's Word? Are you willing to seek God so desperately that nothing else matters? Are you willing to die so that God can really use you?

Mark this: When you decide to go deep, you will tap into a glorious, supernatural realm of God that you have only read about in scriptures. Why play in shallow water, when you can launch into the deep?

Chapter Three

"Launch Out into the Deep!"

"1 And it came to pass, that as the people pressed upon him to hear the word of God, he stood by the lake of Gennesaret, [the sea of Galilee]

2 And saw two ships standing by the lake: but the fishermen were gone out of them, and were washing their nets.

3 And he entered into one of the ships, which was Simon's, and prayed him that he would thrust out a little from the land. And he sat down, and taught the people out of the ship.

4 Now when he had left speaking, he said unto Simon, Launch out into the deep, and let down your nets for a draught.

5 And Simon answering said unto him, Master, we have toiled all the night, and have taken nothing: nevertheless at thy word I will let down the net.

6 And when they had this done, they enclosed a great multitude of fishes: and their net brake.

7 And they beckoned unto their partners, which were in the other ship, that they should come and help them. And they came, and filled both the ships, so that they began to sink."

Luke 5:1-7

Scriptures reveal that multitudes eagerly pressed in to hear the Word of God, BUT we must realize there was a group of fishermen who did not share in the others' enthusiasm. You see, these men had labored all night long... They used every trick of their trade, trying to catch fish... Fishing for them was NOT merely a form of relaxation... No, fishing was their profession... Fishing was how they made their money... And the more fish they caught, the more money they made. These were not men who just decided to hop on a boat one day and take up a new hobby... No, these men came from generations of well-trained and highly skilled fishermen who had passed down the trade. From childhood Simon had practiced his trade, and he had become a very successful fisherman. But on this particular night, Simon couldn't PAY a fish to bite.

The present story most likely takes place sometime during the middle of the day because Simon says that they had been toiling all night. In other words, they had been out on the sea, trying to catch fish, all night long. We must understand that even though it was now the middle of the day, the fisherman's job still wasn't over.

You see, Simon's day didn't end when he returned to shore. Once he was back at shore, nets had to be washed, the boat had to be maintained, supplies had to be restocked, and crews had to be paid. Simon also had to negotiate with merchants and others in the shipping industry... All of this caused fishermen to have long, tiring hours. So, we can imagine that as Jesus ministered to the multitude, Simon and the other fishermen, who were upset, despondent, discouraged and worried about how they were going to pay their bills... they passively listened to Jesus, while occupying themselves in the shallow water.

Even today there are people who occupy themselves in shallow water, refusing to go deep. They've tried all of the tricks of the trade... they've pulled all the strings they could find, but they just can't seem to find resolve. Well, the answer, my friend, is to go deep! I don't care what your issue may be; God has the answer! You may not know how you are going to make ends meet; the doctors may have given you up... everything may seem hopeless... your world may be turned up-side-down!

But I hear God saying, "Launch Out Into the Deep!"

The scripture tells us that when Jesus was finished speaking, He instructed Simon to "Launch out into the deep and let down his nets." Simon responds by saying respectfully, *"Master, we have toiled all night long and have taken nothing."* Now, before we begin to judge Simon because of his back talk, we must realize that Simon was not yet a disciple... he had heard of Jesus' reputation, he had listened to Jesus teach, but he really didn't know who Jesus was... he hadn't had a personal encounter with Jesus. His faith was just a little weak... You see, if Simon's faith had been strong, he would have immediately jumped into the boat, rallied up some of his friend's boats to go with him, and eagerly rowed out into the deep water, expecting a miracle! But instead, we see Simon telling Jesus what he had already done.

In essence, he was saying to Jesus... "This is not going to work! I'm an experienced fisherman, I've been doing this all of my life, my Daddy fished, my Granddaddy fished, my Great Granddaddy fished and they taught me everything they knew. But out of respect for you, Jesus, out of respect for who THEY say you are... I'll take my boat back out into the deep."

I can imagine Simon thinking, I'm exhausted! I haven't slept all night long... I really don't feel like playing games. He probably thought, I just finished cleaning up all of my fishing equipment and I don't feel like going through that again... If I take my boat back out, I'm going to have to pay my crew overtime in order for them to go with me....

Simon may have even thought, If you're really the son of God, why not just speak me some fish into existence.... This just doesn't make sense; why do I have to go back out into the water?

As we read of this encounter, it's easy to question Simon's hesitation: after all, if God said it, Simon should have kept his mouth shut and just done it! But aren't you glad that God looks beyond our faults and sees our needs... Aren't you thankful that God honors your mustard seed faith? Yes, we would all love to have GREAT BIG FAITH, but I'm so glad that God honors a little bit of faith!

Throughout the Bible we see God telling people to do things that just didn't make sense. It didn't make sense to Mary and Martha for Jesus to have them take Him to Lazarus' tomb after their brother had been dead for three days; but the sisters obeyed Jesus and their brother Lazarus rose from the dead! It didn't make sense for Jesus to spit on the ground, make clay and put it into the blind man's eyes and then send him to the pool of Siloam to wash; but the blind man obeyed Jesus and he received his sight! In another passage of scripture, it made no sense to Peter when Jesus told him to cast a hook, take up the first fish that bit and get money out of the fish's mouth; but Peter obeyed and Peter got paid! I can't perceive how my black sins can be washed in red blood and then I become white as snow; but I obeyed God's call, and now, I'm the righteousness of Christ Jesus!

It made no sense to Simon for Jesus to send him back to the same spot he had been in all night long, to do the same things that he had already done; but Simon obeyed Jesus, and because of his obedience, he was able to OPERATE in OVERFLOW! Overflow is available to all of us, but we must obey God!

You don't have to like it... You don't have to agree with it... You don't have to understand it... It may sound crazy… It may cost you something… It may NOT make sense… It may even cause you some discomfort… but if God said it, that settles it! If God spoke it, He will bring it to pass! OBEY GOD… because Your Miracle Depends On It!

The Bible says that as soon as Simon obeyed God's command, they caught a great multitude of fish, so many fish that their net broke. You see, after Simon obeyed God and went deep; he immediately began to operate in OVERFLOW! He had so many fish that he had to call his partners over, who were in other ships, to help him with his overflow! The Bible also says that there were so many fish, that Simon's partners' boat began to sink.

There's another message here and it's this: Don't be stingy… share the goods! Child of God, we must rid ourselves of the STINGY mentality that includes only Me, Myself and I. God blesses you so that you can bless others!

> "Give, and it will be given to you: good
> measure,
> pressed down, shaken together, and running
> over
> will be put into your bosom. For with the same
> measure that you use, it will be measured back
> to you."
> (Luke 6:38)

You must understand that when you operate in OVERFLOW, you will have so much that you won't be able to spend it all by yourself. God is going to supernaturally make some of you millionaires. God is going to bless some of you with more than you've ever had in your life! God is positioning His people in high places. He's putting some in positions of POWER so that His glory can be revealed to the nations! God is going to endow some of you with supernatural spiritual gifts to do great and mighty exploits! God is going to BLOW YOUR MIND!!!

I am amazed at ministries that would rather leave souls to die and go to hell than to work together with other believers outside of their own church. It is an intolerable pride to think that ours is the only ministry that is effectively working in the Kingdom. Some people are envious and afraid that if they help others, those they help might be more successful than they are.   Please understand that we serve A Great Big God, and our Great Big God got a whole lot of stuff; enough stuff for all of us to operate in OVERFLOW!

When Simon Peter saw the overflow of fish, he fell down at Jesus' knees and said, "Depart from me; for I am a sinful man." Simon meant no disrespect, but when he saw how God had blessed him in spite of his doubt, he felt unworthy of the blessing. When Simon realized his sinfulness, and became aware of the Holiness of Jesus, he was overtaken with humility and shame. All of us, even in our unworthy state, have reaped the blessings of God. Most of us, at one time or another, have wondered why God had us do things that just didn't make sense, only to find out afterwards that there was a miracle in our obedience.

For example, somebody was running late for work and God said, Don't get on the highway today; take the long rout; and, although this didn't make sense, she obeyed God, only to find out later that a fatal accident was avoided! Somebody gave their last dime in offering when her rent was past due and, out of nowhere, God stepped in and made a way! Somebody chose to attend a prayer meeting instead of making overtime on the job and that same day was blessed with a brand new car, NO MONEY DOWN! Somebody called the IRS to make arrangements to pay a $3000 debt that was owed the Government and was placed on hold for one hour and fifteen minutes...

Although he wanted to hang up the telephone, God said wait... and when IRS finally got back on the phone... they said, "Our records show that you have a ZERO balance, sir!"

Somebody's doctor told her that she had six months to live, but God said that she would live and not die; and three years later she is a living witness that God is a healer! I didn't make these scenarios up... They are all true testimonies of various believers who have been miraculously blessed by God!

Let me share my son's personal testimony with you. As aforementioned, he spent several years in jail. While in jail, his cellmate offered him some marijuana. Initially, my son refused the offer, but eventually he gave into the temptation. After smoking several puffs, my son realized that he had made a big mistake. Not only did the drug make him sick, his semihigh was disrupted by the prison guards busting into his cell in order to conduct a random drug test. My son was so disoriented that all he could do was cry out to God for mercy!

> "Then they cry out to the LORD in their
> trouble,
> And He brings them out of their distresses."
> Psalms 107:28

You see, if drugs were found in his system, he would be placed in the hole for six months and his jail sentence would be extended. Despite his guilt, my son obeyed God and asked Him for mercy. Now, this made absolutely no sense to my son because the smoke from the weed still filled his cell, and by all accounts he was busted! But my son had enough faith to obey God; he repented, and asked God for mercy. He also made a vow to the Lord never to smoke marijuana again!!!

When the test results came back, my son's cellmate tested positive for drugs and he suffered all of the negative repercussions associated with the crime (six months in the hole and an additional six months added onto his prison sentence). BUT GOD supernaturally cleansed my son's blood stream and his test results came back negative... Not one trace of drugs were found in his system! Don't tell me God won't bring you out! I'm a witness that God will keep you even when you don't have enough sense to keep yourself!

> "For he shall give his angels charge over thee,
> to keep thee in <u>all</u> thy ways."
> (Psalms 91:11)

When you're on the mountain top... He'll keep you! When you're in the valley low... He'll keep you! When you're doing all you know to do... He'll keep you! When you are doing things you know you shouldn't do... He'll keep you! When your faith is great... He'll keep you! When your faith is weak... He'll keep you! In all thy ways, God's got some angels in charge to KEEP you!

Jesus told Simon, "...from hence forth, thou shall catch men." And Simon heeded the call, forsook all and followed Jesus. We must understand that this is our great commission... to forsake all and to be spiritual Catchers of Men. We have been commissioned to take whole nations in our Gospel nets.

> "Ask of me, and I shall give thee the heathen
> for
> thine inheritance, and the uttermost parts of
> the earth for thy possession."
> Psalms 2:8

You may wonder, "Why should I ask for the heathen when I can just ask for the CASH?" Well, we must first realize that human life carries the highest value in the world. The Bible tells us that we were *made in the image of God*, We were *made a little lower than the angles* and that the Lord *gave us dominion over all things*.

Child of God, the Devil even knows your value. Why do you think he works overtime to kill, steal and destroy? You must understand that although cold cash is great, cars, houses, money, jewelry, **none** of these things will go with you when you die. Your true inheritance lies in what you can take with you to eternity. You see, when you die, you will leave all of your worldly possessions.

But every soul that you win into the kingdom is your spiritual inheritance. Every person that is saved as a result of your witness… every soul that you bring into the Kingdom of God will go with you to glory.

Another reason we should ask the Lord to give us the heathen is that some heathen are wealthy!

"…the wealth of the sinner is laid up for the
just."
Proverbs 13:22

Some of us know this scripture as well as we know our own names… we can quote it in our sleep. But may I suggest to you that just reciting this passage will not get you wealth! In order to get the wealth of the sinner, you have to **Go Fishing!!! And you've GOT TO GO DEEP**!

I've heard people debate whether the church should take donations that were won through the lottery. I've heard people say that they would burn the drug dealer's money. For everyone who feels that we shouldn't use the sinner's money, may I suggest to you a more excellent way: Bless the sinner's money and PUT THAT MONEY TO USE IN THE KINGDOM OF GOD! I admonish you to stop hugging the shore and launch out into the deep! Go FISHING!! There's money in the fish's mouth…

"…go to the sea, cast in a hook, and take the fish
that comes up first. And when you have
opened its mouth, you will find a piece of
money;…"
Matthew 17:27

Go get some drug dealers! Go get some prostitutes!
Go get some gamblers! Go get some rappers! Go get some
NFL players! Go get some NBA Players! Go get some
doctors and lawyers! Go get some lottery winners! Go get
some business owners! Go get some actors! Go get some
entrepreneurs AND BRING THEM INTO THE
KINGDOM!!! Stop hating those who have more than you
have... Stop sitting back, wishing you could drive what
they drive and live like they live... THIS IS YOUR
SEASON; THIS IS YOUR TIME FOR OVERFLOW! GO
GET YOUR INHEARITANCE!

I have to tell you that your efforts, in and of
themselves, are pointless; your wisdom and strength are
insufficient. The secret to success in Christian work is to
be guided by the Lord. And sometimes He will have you
do things that just don't make sense. Trust God even
when it seems you're simply occupying shallow water.

You may be attending church religiously, but there's
still a void. You may be reading the Bible, but you still feel
discouraged. You may be praying all night long, but
you're still despondent. Don't allow your circumstances
to distract you from what God has purposed for your life.
I don't care what your struggle is: keep holding on to the
promises of God!

> "And let us not be weary in well doing:
> for in due season we shall reap, if we faint not."
> Galatians 6:9

I hear someone saying, "I work in the church, I pay
my tithes, I'm doing all I know to live right; when will my
ship roll in?"

> "Therefore, my beloved brethren, be ye stedfast,
> unmoveable, always abounding in the
> WORK of the Lord, forasmuch as ye
> know that your labour is not in vain in the
> Lord."

(1Corinthians 15:58)

This is your season! Go possess your inheritance! Stop hugging the shore! Launch out into the deep! You're Overflow is ON THE WAY!

Chapter Four

Power in God's Word

"Jesus Christ the same yesterday,
and to day, and for ever."
(Hebrews 13:8)

God never changes! His supernatural power is still available today for anyone who is willing to sacrifice and GO DEEP! Every believer's hope should be to really know God!

"That I may know him,
and the power of his resurrection,
and the fellowship of his sufferings,
being made conformable unto his death;"
Philippians 3:10

The only way to live a life of purpose and to fulfill the destiny that God had planned for you before the foundation of the world is to know God. When you embark upon a life of dedicated prayer in the Holy Spirit, God will reveal himself to you… He will reveal to you His nature and His mind.

"For he that speaketh in an unknown tongue
speaketh not unto men, but unto God:
for no man understandeth him;
howbeit in the spirit he speaketh mysteries."
1Corinthians 14:2

When you pray in the Holy Spirit, you are praying the mysteries of God; you are praying the mind of God. When you pray the mind of God you are praying the perfect will of God for your life, your family, the nation and the world.

> "Just as He chose us in Him before the
> foundation of the world, that we should be holy
> and without blame before Him in love, having
> predestined us to adoption as sons by Jesus
> Christ to Himself, according to the good
> pleasure of His will"
> Ephesians 1:4-5

We all have desires, likes, dislikes, opinions, etc., but our prayers can't be governed by our emotions. We must learn to adopt the attitude that Jesus Christ had when He prayed in the Garden of Gethsemane, saying, "...*nevertheless not My will, but Yours, be done*" *(Luke 22:42)*

In order to walk out our destiny, we must be totally open and totally yielded to God. We must pray the mind of Christ so that He can instruct us and show us what our destiny and our purpose is. This type of prayer requires FAITH!

> "Now faith is the substance of things hoped for,
> the evidence of things not seen."
> Hebrews 11:1

Faith allows you to see into the spirit realm. Bishop John Francis puts it like this:

> "What your spirit picks up in the spirit realm is
> the substance, or the essence of your miracle.
> Now here is the thing, the atmosphere that you
> surround your faith with, will determine the
> manifestation of your blessing. H_2O is a
> substance, but the condition of the atmosphere
> changes its manifestation. When H_2O is hot, it
> creates Steam (the vapor phase)... when it's
> frozen, it creates Ice (the solid phase)... and
> when it's temperate, it creates Water (the liquid

phase).   So the question is, what atmosphere
should we surround our faith with? The
answer is 'Works!'"

"For as the body without the spirit is dead,
so faith without works is dead also."
James 2:26

"Seest thou how faith wrought with his works,
and by works was faith made perfect?"
(James 2:22)

Faith must be surrounded by works. Now, what
might those works be? Consider the following scriptures:

"And whatsoever we ask, we receive of him,
because we keep his commandments,
and do those things that are pleasing in his
sight."
1John 3:22

"Therefore I say unto you, What things soever
ye desire, when ye pray, believe that ye receive
them,
and ye shall have them."
Mark 11:24

Your faith must be surrounded by a holy lifestyle,
obedience to God's Word and prayer.   An unholy
atmosphere will kill faith and prevent your breakthrough.
Listen, the people you surround yourself with can either
foster or kill your faith. Consider the following passage of
scripture:

"And, behold, there came a man named Jairus,
and
he was a ruler of the synagogue: and he fell
down at

Jesus' feet, and besought him that he would come into his house:
For he had one only daughter, about twelve years of age, and she lay a dying. But as he went the people thronged him….."
Luke 8:41-42

"While he yet spake, there cometh one from the ruler of the synagogue's house, saying to him, Thy daughter is dead; trouble not the Master. But when Jesus heard it, he answered him, saying,
Fear not: believe only, and she shall be made whole.
And when he came into the house, he suffered no man to go in, save Peter, and James, and John, and the father and the mother of the maiden.
And all wept, and bewailed her: but he said, Weep not; she is not dead, but sleepeth.
And they laughed him to scorn, knowing that she was dead.
And he put them all out, and took her by the hand,
and called, saying, Maid, arise.
And her spirit came again, and she arose straightway: and he commanded to give her meat."
Luke 8:49-55

As we examine these scriptures we see that Jairus had a measure of faith. Jairus was a minister in a synagogue or place of worship. He sought out Jesus to come and heal his dying daughter. We must understand that many of the priests and scribes, his peers if you will, didn't acknowledge Jesus as Lord; in fact, most of them thought that Jesus was blaspheming against God for allowing people to worship Him as the Messiah. Therefore, for Jairus to ask for Jesus' help and openly fall at Jesus' feet, took faith.

Now Jairus' faith caught the attention of Jesus and He consented to go to Jairus' house. Don't let anyone tell you that you can't have faith for others. I don't know how many times I have heard this scripture quoted as an excuse for unanswered prayers: Matthew 9:29 says, "... According to your faith be it unto you." Listen, your faith can change lives... faith can still raise the dead... faith can still open blinded eyes... faith can save your children....your faith can snatch the prostitute off the corner... your faith can take the taste for drugs and alcohol away from your son's mouth...

Before Jesus could get to Jairus' house, someone comes bearing bad news. Remember, faith must have the proper atmosphere in order to produce the desired results. Jesus realizes at this point that Jairus' faith was weakened by the news of his daughter's death, so Jesus tells Jairus to fear not and believe only. Here we see that there is no place for fear when one is exercising faith. Fear cancels out faith and ushers in disbelief. Doubt will ultimately strip your power and render you helpless.

"For God hath not given us the spirit of fear;
but of
power, and of love, and of a sound mind."
2 Timothy 1:7

Jairus had faith enough to believe that God could heal his daughter, but he didn't have enough faith to believe that God could raise her from the dead. When Jairus was made aware of what had happened in the natural realm (the death of his daughter), he left the spirit realm (faith) and began to fear, which caused him to doubt. Notice also that the person who brought the bad news to Jairus says in essence, "It's too late now, tell Jesus don't even bother to come."

Jairus was fine until he received the news. This is a good place for me to tell you to be careful to whom you listen. You can't take counsel from everybody. They may be authorities in their respective fields, bankers, lawyers, doctors, but if they don't have faith in God, if they can't go beyond what they see in the natural, what they've learned educationally, what's been proven scientifically – if they don't believe what God said – then don't take any stock in their counsel.

When Jesus arrived at Jairus' house, He found a multitude of people. In that day it was customary for mourners to gather around the deceased. At the moment of death, weeping and wailing began and continued without intermission until the deceased was buried. So, as Jesus approached the house, He was faced with a loud uproar and frantic demonstrations of sorrow.

No doubt there were also some who were simply curiosity seekers who wanted to witness what Jesus was going to do inside the house, but Jesus would allow only a select few into the house. Here we see that in order for your faith to produce desired results, you must surround yourself with people of like faith. Jesus sifted through the multitude and selected five people to enter into the house with Him. He chose the people with the greatest amount of faith.

He selected His disciples because they had seen Him perform miracles in the past, and He chose the dead girl's parents because he knew they really wanted to see their only daughter restored. Although they all possessed the potential for like faith, they wavered when they saw the child lying lifeless, for the Bible said that they all cried... Not only did they cry, they bewailed (a long, loud, high-pitched cry of grief and pain).

Jesus realized their faith was weak, so He said, "Weep not..." In other words, don't look at the natural circumstances, look at me... focus on what you know in your heart I can do. It's OK to come to Jesus with tears for His Word says: **"They that sow in tears shall reap in joy" (Psalms 126:5).** But don't keep crying over the same situation. At a certain point, you need to stop crying, throw your shoulders back, look up, suck it up and joyfully await the manifestation of your miracle!

> "Thus saith the LORD; Refrain thy voice from
> weeping, and thine eyes from tears: for thy
> work shall be rewarded, saith the LORD..."
> Jeremiah 31:16

Focus on Jesus and His promises.... Stop crying about your children... focus on God's promise!

> "And in thy seed shall all the nations of the
> earth be
> blessed; because thou hast obeyed my voice"
> Genesis 22:18

> "And all thy children shall be taught of the
> LORD;
> and great shall be the peace of thy children"
> Isaiah 54:13

Stop worrying about your finances, focus on the Word of God!

> "For ye know the grace of our Lord Jesus
> Christ, that, though he was rich, yet for your
> sakes he became poor, that ye through his
> poverty might be rich"
> 2Corinthians 8:9

> "Let them shout for joy, and be glad, that
> favour my righteous cause: yea, let them say

> continually, Let the LORD be magnified, which
> hath pleasure in the prosperity of his servant."
> Psalms 35:27

It's time to stop crying about your problems like a wimpy, jelly-backed coward and take authority over the adversity through the **Word of God**! Remember when Jesus was tempted by the devil while He was in the mountains? He overcame every temptation by quoting the Word of God! FOCUS ON THE WORD!

> "Then was Jesus led up of the Spirit into the
> wilderness to be tempted of the devil."
> Matthew 4:1

Jesus gave us a perfect example of the way to resist temptation and to confuse the tempter. We must realize that God often leads His servants into great trials and tribulations in order to prepare them for the awesome task He has commissioned them to accomplish. In fact, the individual who is blessed with divine favor and spiritual gifts should expect extra persecution.

> "And lest I should be exalted above measure by
> the abundance of the revelations, a thorn in the
> flesh was given to me, a messenger of Satan to
> buffet me, lest I be exalted above measure."
> 2 Corinthians 12:7

Paul had a messenger of Satan sent to buffet him after he had been in the third heaven. The Devil has a particular spite against highly anointed people who are committed to serving God. The moment you decide to give your life wholly to God, look out because the enemy is headed your way. The devil tries to shake our faith in God by causing us to question the relevance of God's Word. After all, Satan's job is to oppose truth.

> "…when he speaks a lie, he speaks from his
> own resources, for he is a liar and the father of
> it."
> John 8:44

Following each high moment expect a low moment to follow; after every blessing expect a trial. When your soul is enriched, turmoil is lurking somewhere in the future. Realizing this, we must learn how to repel the enemy with prayer. Just as light draws insects, bugs and mosquitoes, the light of the anointing will draw the enemy. Prayer is the spiritual repellent that will keep the sting of the enemy away. Yes, the adversary will still be lured to the anointing, but his power to insert his poisonous venom will be sapped!!

> "Behold, I give unto you power to tread on
> serpents
> and scorpions, and over all the power of the
> enemy: and nothing shall by any means hurt
> you."
> Luke 10:19

The only offensive weapon in our Christian armory is the Word of God, for the Word is the Sword of the Spirit. Consider the following scriptures:

> "And when he had fasted forty days and forty
> nights, he was afterward an hungred.
> And when the tempter came to him, he said, If
> thou be the Son of God, command that these
> stones be made bread.
> But he answered and said, **It is written**, Man
> shall
> not live by bread alone, but by every word that
> proceedeth out of the mouth of God.
> Then the devil taketh him up into the holy city,
> and setteth him on a pinnacle of the temple,
> And saith unto him, If thou be the Son of God,

cast thyself down: for it is written, He shall give
his angels charge concerning thee: and in their
hands
they shall bear thee up, lest at any time thou
dash thy foot against a stone.
 Jesus said unto him, **It is written** again, Thou
shalt not tempt the Lord thy God.
 Again, the devil taketh him up into an
exceeding
high mountain, and sheweth him all the
kingdoms
of the world, and the glory of them;
 And saith unto him, All these things will I give
thee,
if thou wilt fall down and worship me.
 Then saith Jesus unto him, **Get thee hence,
Satan**:
for **it is written**, Thou shalt worship the Lord
thy God, and him only shalt thou serve.
 Then the devil leaveth him, and, behold, angels
came and ministered unto him."
Matthew 4:2-11

When you decide to face down and press into God,
He will fill you with His peace and endow you with
supernatural revelation. During these times of infilling,
the devil will attempt to infuse you with pride and vain
self-conceit. You will be tempted to do things that will
ultimately bring you low, and lead you to sin. This is why
you must know the Word of God and keep it ever present
in your heart.

"Your word I have hidden in my heart,
That I might not sin against You!"
Ps 119:11

Jesus Himself fought with no other weapon. He
certainly could have spoken new revelations, but he chose

to say, "It is written." The Word of God carries a power that even the devil cannot deny. You can talk until you are blue in the face, you can pray the most eloquent prayer that has ever been prayed, you can travail long, loud and hard, but if you're not speaking God's Word, you are not shaking the devil's camp. You must speak the Word of God! You must continue to release the WORD OF GOD into the atmosphere.

The Word of God is the only thing that scares the enemy. Your words don't faze the devil. He speaks and understands every human language known to man. But the devil is no match for God's Word nor God's language!

"Death and life are in the power of the
tongue..."
Proverbs 18:21

Focus on what God has said in His Word! Speak The Word! Stop begging God and begin thanking Him for what He has already done in the Spirit! Stop focusing on what you can see...

"While we look not at the things which are
seen,
but at the things which are not seen: for the
things
which are seen are temporal; but the things
which
are not seen are eternal."
2 Corinthians 4:18

God told Jairus and the others "Weep not; she is not dead, but sleepeth".

But they didn't focus on the Word of God, which is life; they focused on what the situation looked like: death. The Bible says that their disbelief was so bad that they scorned Jesus (rejected Him with contempt) because they knew (beyond doubt) the child was dead. At this point, there was absolutely no faith present, not even mustard seed faith; so Jesus puts them all out of the house!

Here is the message… Whomever you have in your life that refuses to believe God's Word, cut them loose! I don't care if you've been friends for 30 years, if your friends are causing you to doubt what God has promised you, let them go! If your family refuses to believe God is with you, they've got to go. Don't stop loving them and praying for them, but you must distance yourself from everyone who is causing you to doubt God!

> "Which things also we speak, not in the words
> which man's wisdom teacheth, but which the
> Holy Ghost teacheth; comparing spiritual
> things with spiritual"
> 1Corinthians 2:13

The man or woman who does not possess the Spirit of God cannot completely comprehend nor receive the things of the Spirit. To them, spiritual things are considered foolishness because they have no spiritual mind. Without the Spirit to lead and guide, man is forced to function within the sphere of normality… But we serve a God that specializes in the sphere of the IMPOSSIBLE! All you have to do is create the proper atmosphere for the miraculous to take place. Notice what happens when Jesus gets rid of all of the unbelievers….

He took the child by the hand, said "Maid, arise," and immediately her spirit entered into her body once again. Watch what Jesus did: He rebuked all unbelief, and took authority over the environment. Once the atmosphere was conducive to a miracle, He made a demand on His faith. Then He reached into the spirit realm, snatched the spirit of Jarius' daughter, brought it back into the natural sphere, placed it back into the child's body and commanded her to get up!

He didn't scream and holler, He didn't shake, rattle and roll, He didn't sweat and cry all night long in prayer, He didn't call her name a zillion times... He simply prepared the atmosphere for a miracle and spoke His desire into fruition.

Chapter Five

Beauty, Within and Without!

"Whose adorning let it not be that outward
adorning of plaiting the hair, and of
wearing of gold, or of putting on of apparel;
But let it be the hidden man of the heart,
in that which is not corruptible, even the
ornament
of a meek and quiet spirit, which is in the
sight of God of great price."
1 Peter 3:3-4

The mental image of beauty varies from person to person, from culture to culture, from age to age, and from season to season. What may be beautiful in other parts of the world may not be considered beautiful in America. In Africa some of the tribal women have drastically stretched their ear lobes by hanging heavy wooden earrings from them; to them this is considered beautiful. Some African tribes wear wooden sticks through their noses; this is considered beautiful to them.

In parts of the Middle East, women must be totally covered up from head to toe and only their eyes can show; to them, this exemplifies class and beauty. Even in America, the concept of beauty differs. Some think that spiked, royal blue hair is beautiful; others like straight silky hair, while still others prefer the thick curly look. Some want to be skinny, while the skinny are trying to gain weight; Yes, everyone has their own opinion of what is beautiful. The familiar cliché, "Beauty is in the eyes of the beholder" has proven to be an accurate statement.

Cosmetic companies are making millions of dollars on skin care and hair care products. Beauty supply establishments sell hair weaves, fake eyelashes and all sorts of products to enhance the outward appearance. People today have many options.

If they weren't born with long hair, they can buy some. If they don't have naturally long fingernails, they can have some sculpted on. If they are overweight and can't seem to discipline themselves to eat correctly, they can have gastro-bypass surgery and lose weight quickly. If they don't like the shape of their nose, they can look in a catalogue and pick out another, more appealing one. If their breasts are too small, they can enlarge them; if their stomach is too big, they can have it tucked.

Yes, people are obsessed with their outward appearance and, if they have enough money or the right kind of insurance, they can literally transform their outer appearance.

While many people are spending millions of dollars on their outer man, little attention is given to their inner man. Tremendous emphasis is placed on impressing the world, but little concern is given to how we look in the sight of God. We are becoming more self-absorbed and falling further away from God. Because the world is full of various standards of beauty, keeping up with each standard of outward beauty is an impossible task. Therefore, greater emphasis needs to be placed on the inner man and the first point that needs to be addressed is the importance of being secure and content in WHO YOU ARE, and in WHOSE YOU ARE!

The devil will try to speak insecurity into your spirit. He'll tell you that you're ugly, you're fat, your nose is too big, you're stupid or you're not good enough. He'll try to make you believe that the abuse and struggle you have endured have permanently scarred you, preventing you from accomplishing your purpose. Well, the devil is a liar because God said that you were made in His image and in His likeness, and that you are fearfully and wonderfully made!

The problem with some of us is that we don't really understand who we are, not in our own flesh, but who we are because of Christ. We are **the** King's kids; notice I said THE King's kids because beside Him there is no other! You haven't taken hold of the fact that you are royalty! You don't realize that the beauty of the Lord is upon you! Stop looking to the world for a standard of beauty and ask God to establish within you your own sense of style, elegance, poise and grace; a style that will bring God glory and honor!

I'm looking for the day when the world will look to the church for style. I'm looking for the time when in corporate America two women can have on the same suit, but the one who's a child of God just wears hers better... And the Sinner says to the Saint, "Girl, we have on the same suit, we're the same size... why does your suit look so much better on you then mine does?" And the Saint replies, "Because it's not about the suit, baby, it's all about the God in me!" When God rests, rules and abides in your spirit, you can't help but look good!

Have you ever seen some of your old grade school or high school classmates and they see you and marvel about how young you look? Some of them look twice their age; they look hard and beat up, while you're still walking around looking like a teenager. That's because sin will beat you up! But there is true beauty in walking with the Lord!

Instead of accepting your friends' compliments by saying, "Thank you, you know I get plenty of sleep, I exercise and I take my vitamins every day..." you need to take that opportunity to tell the sinner man, "I look this way because God has preserved me! The things I used to do, I don't do any more... The places I used to go, I don't go any more... The sinful desires that I used to have, God took them away, and the grace of God has beautified me with salvation!"

Many conservative religious sects have literally misunderstood 1 Peter 3:3. Some Christians have taken this scripture to mean that saints should not braid their hair, wear jewelry, or even dress fashionably. This concept allowed self-righteousness to creep into the church, for it gave some a measuring stick whereby to judge the spirituality of the saints. In other words, a person's spirituality was based totally on their outward appearance.

Years ago, back in the 40's and 50's, some people didn't believe that saints should wear bright colors. Others were against applying chemicals to the hair, and women certainly couldn't cut their hair. Wearing wigs, heal- and toe-out shoes, and even wedding rings were all sins.

When two saints were married, they had to exchange watches. That's right: back in the 40's couples had to exchange watches instead of rings. My mother and father had been married for many years prior to her joining the Apostolic church. My father was not Apostolic and he didn't understand the correlation between wedding rings and sin. But, in order to keep Mom out of hell, Dad went along with the program and allowed Mom to take off her wedding ring. Now here's where it gets crazy... Some years later, when the religious hierarchy decided that rings weren't a sin after all, wouldn't you know it –my mother wanted a brand new wedding ring.

I am my parent's youngest child, the only girl, and the apple of my father's eye. Historically, I have been able to get anything I desire out of my dad. Therefore, I was not surprised when my mom put me up to asking my dad to buy her a new wedding ring for Christmas. Although I had my dad wrapped around my little finger, getting things from him was not an "ask and immediately receive" process. I usually had to implement the art of persuasion in order to get my way. So, I was left with the difficult task of trying to explain to my father how God had changed his mind about his children wearing wedding rings....

This was a difficult task because my father and I would always debate scripture. I was constantly on my father about being baptized in Jesus' Name and receiving the Holy Ghost. Even as a young child I loved the Lord, and I knew in whom I believed and I wanted my daddy, whom I truly loved also, to be saved!

A great deal of my life was spent trying to get my daddy to interpret the scriptures the way I did. Dad and I would actually argue over the scriptures. He'd throw things at me like, "How are Jesus and God one, when Jesus prayed to His father?" and I would come right back at him with scriptures like what Jesus said to Philip, *"He that hath seen me, hath seen the Father."* Although I was a child, I did a pretty good job of holding my own.

This is a good place for me to tell you, don't underestimate young people. They understand more than you think they do. Just keep making spiritual deposits into their lives; keep them in church, keep them in the Word of God, keep praying for them and when the enemy rises against them, they will have a well of living water from which to draw.

Don't allow the enemy to use your children to incite discouragement and fear. Stand firm on the Word of God and use His precious promises as a means of building your faith.

> "And it shall come to pass in the last days, says God, That I will pour out of My Spirit on all flesh;
> your sons and your daughters shall prophesy,

your young men shall see visions..."
Acts 2:17

"Your seed I will establish forever...."
Psalms 89:4

"All your children shall be taught by the LORD,
And great shall be the peace of your children."
Isaiah 54:13

I don't care what the situation looks like... I don't care what it sounds like... I don't care what the circumstances are...

"Heaven and earth will pass away, but my
words will by no means pass away."
Matthew 24:35

Please don't give up on your children. Stand on the promises of God. You see, when I was a child, I didn't understand everything that was in the scripture, but I had enough of God's Word in me to be able to come back at my father every time he tried to convince me that the Holy Ghost wasn't necessary. Each time he tried to convince me that speaking in tongues wasn't necessary, I'd come back with, "Daddy I've already got the Holy Ghost and YOU CAN'T TELL ME WHAT I GOT – ISN'T REAL!"

Even in the natural sense, there are things you can't tell me aren't real. It's too late to tell me that my comfortable recliner won't hold me; I've already sat in it, and I didn't fall down. It's too late to tell me that the food at my favorite restaurant is nasty; I've already tasted their food, and it is good! It's too late to tell me that my automobile won't transport me where I need to go; I drive it every day! There are just certain things the devil can't speak into my spirit. I hope you see where I'm going with this!

It's too late to tell me that God can't keep me; He's already holding me in the cradle of His arms! It's too late to tell me that God isn't good; I've already tasted and seen that the LORD is good! It's too late to tell me that God can't take me where I need to go; He's already directing my path!

So when I didn't know the correct scriptures to quote to my father, I just stood on my personal experience... I stood on my testimony... and before he passed away, my father was baptized in Jesus' name and he received the gift of the Holy Ghost evidenced by speaking in other tongues!!!

"And they overcame him by the blood of the Lamb
and by the word of their testimony..."
Revelation 12:11

It's all right if you pause at this point and take a praise break for what God did for me. I'm certain that you have family members and friends that you want God to save. When you rejoice with others in their victory, God will shift you right into your own victory! Because of the blood of Jesus, you can walk in victory! All you need is faith, the Word of God and your testimony! When the enemy speaks defeat to your spirit, you tell him, "Whatsoever I do shall prosper!" When the devil afflicts your body, you tell him, "God said I am the LORD that healeth thee!" When Satan causes you to fear, you say, "No weapon that is formed against me shall prosper!"

If you don't get anything else, get a personal testimony and some Word in your belly to stand on! Don't let the devil back you up in a corner! Turn the Word of God loose on him! You see, your opinion may change, your concept may differ from time to time, but the Word of God remains the same! Stick to the Word of God... it's reliable and it won't change!

With that said, let's continue exploring the topic of this chapter, "Spiritual Beauty." The concept of beauty in the church was once frowned upon. In fact, some thought that the more plainly you dressed and the more homely you appeared, the more holy you were. As I reminisce about my childhood, I can remember that the meanest saints seemed to be the ones that looked the holiest. Can I just be honest?

The old mother with the kinky, nappy hair, the thick light brown stockings, no make-up (not even powder), the one who wore dresses that were down to her ankles, blouses that were buttoned up to her neck (with a scarf on top of that), and sleeves that were down to her wrist... she was mean as a junkyard dog!

I can remember another mother of the church who never smiled and never had anything pleasant to say to the young people. When she saw me at church, she always had a tissue ready to wipe the Vaseline off of my lips (and it definitely **was not** lipstick because my mother wasn't letting me out of the house with lipstick on). In fact, I thought I was really doing something by wearing Vaseline.

I also remember a church deacon bringing a ruler to church in order to measure the length of the girl's skirts and the length of the boy's afros. You see, the *church law* was that the girl's skirts couldn't be too short, and the boy's hair couldn't be too long. So, before the young people went into the choir box to sing with the Junior Choir, they had to be thoroughly checked out. My how times have changed!

Anyway, my point is this: The very ones in the church who were supposed to be the most saved were the ones who were unpleasant and mean-spirited. My grandma told me that, "**PRETTY IS AS PRETTY DOES,**" and down through the years I have found that statement to be true. Some of those very saints who looked the part on the outside, the ones that operated by traditional rules and regulations… they were often the ones who lacked love and compassion.

> "He that loveth not, knoweth not God; for God is love."
> 1 John 4:8

As we read 1 Peter 3:4, we see that God is instructing us not to place our concept of beauty on the corruptible. Clothes, jewelry, your hair style, your made-up face, your sculptured nails, your toned body – everything that the world looks at in order to judge beauty – all of this is corruptible and will soon pass away. True beauty is based on the condition of your heart and how much of God you exemplify.

> "…for the LORD seeth not as man seeth; for man
> looketh on the outward appearance, but the LORD looketh on the heart."
> 1 Samuel 16:7

You see, it really don't matter what you look like to me; what matters is what God sees when He looks at you! God is looking for 1) the beauty of gentleness, 2) the beauty of peace, 3) the beauty of contentment, 4) the beauty of joy, and 5) the beauty of holiness.

God is looking for SANCTIFICATION, He is searching for RIGHTEOUSNESS!

What the world considers beautiful changes from year to year… clothing styles, hair styles, shoe styles… they all change… even though if you hold on to your things a few years, the styles seem to just come right back around.

Although opinions of outer beauty will differ, there is a beauty that transcends every nation and nationality – every creed and color – it transcends every gender! This beauty starts on the inside and illuminates from the inside out.

> "Honour and majesty are before him:
> strength and beauty are in his sanctuary."
> Psalms 96:6

True Beauty can only be found in God! This kind of beauty is everlasting!

In the same way we are born with certain genetic predispositions, such as blue eyes, curly hair, high waist, short stature, we are also born with certain spiritual dispositions.

The Bible tells us that we are all born in sin and shaped in iniquity; therefore, we must realize the need for internal restoration "...and have no confidence in the flesh" (Philippians 3:3). External beauty treatments may fail. You can spend thousands and thousands of dollars and years later the effects of the surgeries are gone! All the pain and discomfort was to no avail because true, everlasting beauty only comes from God!

Several years ago I used to host a health and beauty segment on WPZZ Radio called, **"Barb's Beauty Tips."** During this segment I would give the listening audience various suggestions for enhancing their physical well-being and their outward appearance. I am the health editor for the Christian Outlook, an international publication of the Pentecostal Assemblies of the World. The health articles that I write stress the importance of consuming a healthy diet and exercising, but the tips that I am about to give you are more valuable than any health and beauty plan I could devise.

BEAUTY TIPS

1. Instead of a **face lift** … "Lift up your heads, O ye gates; and be ye lift up, ye everlasting doors; and the King of glory shall come in. …" "Psalms 24:7

2. Instead of a **makeover consultation**, ask God to… "Create in me a clean heart, O God; and renew a right spirit within me." Psalms 51:10

3. Instead of **liposuction…** ask God to suck out everything that is not like Him… "Search me, O God, and know my heart: try me, and know my thoughts:" (Psalm 139:23)

> "And when you find things that shouldn't be,
> Take them out and strengthen me!
> I must be saved, I must be right,
> I gotta BE WHOLE!"

"O worship the LORD in the beauty of holiness: fear before him, all the earth." Psalms 96:9

Having read this scripture for years, I never fully understood it's full meaning. I asked the Lord what is the beauty of holiness, and **He said the beauty of holiness is that "YOU CANT LOSE…"** So, when you worship the Lord in the beauty of holiness, you worship Him with the confidence that you can't lose. You worship Him in victory. You worship Him in triumph.

It's so important that you get exactly what God is saying here. To drive it home, imagine this:

You are at a basketball game… it's the fourth quarter with one minute left before the game is over, and the score is 40 to 30. The team that has 40 points is smiling from ear to ear… their team players on the bench are hugging each other, their fans in the bleachers are standing up screaming and throwing confetti… they're all celebrating VICTORY even though no one has officially won the game. But the team with 40 points can still celebrate because they know there is absolutely no way that their opponents can get 10 points in one minute and they don't even have possession of the ball.

You see, even though they still have to finish the game, they can celebrate because they KNOW THERE IS NO WAY THEY CAN LOSE! The beauty of holiness is just like that! THE BEAUTY OF HOLINESS IS THAT YOU can celebrate in the midst of the struggle, because there is no way you can LOSE! You have peace in the midst of the storm... You have joy in the midst of sorrow... You have hope when things seem hopeless BECAUSE YOU KNOW THERE IS NO WAY YOU CAN LOOSE!

In 2Chronicles 20:21-22 Jehoshaphat appointed singers to praise the Beauty of Holiness. As I researched this story, I found that all of the odds were against Jehoshaphat and Judah. Mighty armies were coming against them and, in the natural sense, there was no way they could stand against their enemies. But God told Jehoshaphat, You will **not** have to fight this battle. Stand firm and see the deliverance the Lord will give you. All Judah had to do was **have Faith, and Worship and Praise the Beauty of Holiness!**

The Bible says that when they began to sing praises to God, God set ambushes against their enemies and their enemies actually destroyed each other. Not only were their enemies defeated, but the Israelites got all of their enemy's wealth ... The Israelites got so much that they couldn't carry it all at one time. It took them three days to carry all of the spoil away.

But wait, there's more... Not only did they receive great wealth and defeat their enemies, but they also obtained respect from all of the kingdoms of the countries, for the word spread all over the nations of how the God of Israel had fought for them! **YES...The beauty of holiness**

is that You Can't Lose... and when you win, you win BIG!

The beauty of holiness is similar to what the Apostle Paul said. He said that he could be content in whatever situation he found himself because he knew that he couldn't lose! All you've got to do is Worship God in the Beauty of Holiness, realizing that whatever you need is already done in the spirit! You just have to worship God until your blessings manifest! The beauty of holiness will show up through your praise!

Through your praise you will defeat your enemy! Through your praise you will see your family saved! Your praise will loose strong holds! Your praise will open doors that have been shut in your face! Your praise will put money in your bank account!

Your praise will put a new car in your driveway! Your praise will get you into a brand new house! Your praise will get you a raise on your job! Your praise will usher you into your destiny! Your praise will make your gifts known!

We must praise God in the Beauty of Holiness! The beauty of holiness is the righteousness of Christ Jesus! The world should be able to look at our lives and see the beauty of holiness.

> "And be found in him, not having mine own
> righteousness, which is of the law, but that
> which
> is through the faith of Christ, the righteousness
> which is of God by faith:"
> Philippians 3:9

When you operate in the beauty of holiness, when you operate in righteousness, right living, right thinking, right speaking, right actions... you are beautiful and you are victorious! We go to the mirror to see our image, and to gauge if we are beautiful, to see if everything is in place.

Most of us wouldn't leave the house without looking in the mirror at least once to check things out. The very time I rush out of the house without looking in the mirror, I get out and notice a run in my stockings, or a wrinkle that I should have ironed out.

Well, the Word of God is our spiritual mirror. We must gauge our actions, our thoughts, our conversations, our feelings, our relationships, by the Word of God. Don't miss a day without checking yourself out in the WORD. Allow God to show you things that need to be fixed before you go out and represent Him. And when God can see His image in you, you will have true BEAUTY WITHIN AND WITHOUT!

Chapter Six

Deeper Yet I Pray

"Pride goeth before destruction, and an
haughty spirit before a fall. "
Proverbs 16:18

As we press into God and He begins to endow us
with greater anointing and revelation, we must be careful
not to become proud and boastful. God will not tolerate
pride! We must always remember where our blessings
come from and be careful to never take the credit that
belongs only to God!

"For who makes you differ from another? And
what do you have that you did not receive?
Now if you did indeed receive it, why do you
boast as if you had not received it?"
1Corinthians 4:7

Whatever degrees you have earned, whatever gifts
and talents you possess, all of your worldly possessions,
every level you have risen to – never forget that God gave
it to you. It's by the grace of God that you are where you
are today! You must be careful not to embrace man's
compliments and words of adoration. People will cause
you to believe that you are more than you really are.
When people praise you for a job well done, "don't believe
the hype!" Transfer all praise back to your heavenly
Father; because you are nothing, would have nothing, and
could do nothing without Him!

The Apostle Paul wrote the following passage of
scripture concerning pride and the last days:

"In the last days… men shall be lovers of their

own selves, covetous, boasters, proud,
blasphemers,
disobedient to parents, unthankful, unholy,
3 Without natural affection, trucebreakers,
false accusers, incontinent, fierce, despisers of
those that are good,
4 Traitors, heady, highminded, lovers of
pleasures more than lovers of God;
5 Having a form of godliness, but denying the
power thereof: from such turn away.
2Timothy 3:2-5

The spirit of Pride is so subtle that it will sneak up on you before you are even aware of it. You must constantly ask God to show you, *YOU*. Examine your weekly schedule... You may go to church on Sunday, attend Bible study during the week, and even attend a weekly prayer meeting; but compare that to how much time you spend on YOU. Calculate the time you spend each week watching TV, in the beauty shop, in the shopping mall, before the mirror.... Now compare that to the amount of time you spend with God.

When you decide to face down and press deeper into God, one of the main areas He will begin to work on is your pride. The following scriptures vividly illustrate the dangers associated with pride.

30 "The king spake, and said, Is not this great
Babylon, that I have built for the house of the
kingdom by the might of my power, and for the
honour of my majesty?
31 While the word was in the king's mouth,
there fell a voice from heaven, saying, O king
Nebuchadnezzar, to thee it is spoken; The
kingdom is departed from thee.
32 And they shall drive thee from men, and thy
dwelling shall be with the beasts of the field:

they shall make thee to eat grass as oxen, and
seven times shall pass over thee, until thou
know that the most High ruleth in the kingdom
of men, and giveth it to whomsoever he will.
33 The same hour was the thing fulfilled upon
Nebuchadnezzar: and he was driven from men,
and did eat grass as oxen, and his body was wet
with the dew of heaven, till his hairs were
grown like eagles' feathers, and his nails like
birds' claws."
Daniel 4:30-33

In this fourth chapter of Daniel we read about Nebuchadnezzar, the King of Babylon, and his massive wealth. It is during this period that the King defeated and took control of Syria, Phoenicia, Judea, Egypt, and Arabia. So that we might clearly understand the magnitude of his accomplishments, we must acknowledge that science began in Egypt and Babylon with the birth of mathematics, anatomy and astronomy. To the Babylonians we owe the exact measurements of the lunar and solar systems and the tracing of the paths of the planets. History records the existence of beautiful architectural structures and huge libraries with books classified on all subjects.

Yes, Babylon was a very prestigious and powerful nation and King Nebuchadnezzar was in charge of it all. Nebuchadnezzar was the most influential leader of the world at that time, and the Bible says the king was puffed up with pride. He was arrogant… He had a BIG EGO…

We see in our text that King Nebuchadnezzar had been fighting for years, and finally he was in the position where the scripture says that, "He was at rest in his house"… He didn't fear any man… There was no one greater than he was… He had unimaginable wealth and power…He was untouchable…People waited on him hand and foot…Whatever he desired was at his immediate disposal... He was surrounded by a lot of yes men... people who would only tell him what he wanted to hear.

I can imagine them saying...You're such a GREAT King... You're such a FINE King... You're so STRONG a King... You're so SMART a King... There is nobody like you, King!

Listen, don't get it twisted...These people knew what the King was really like. They knew that the king was proud, arrogant and haughty, but they only told the King what he wanted to hear! This is a message in itself and the message is, "Don't Believe the HYPE!" Your flesh wants to hear how good you look... Your flesh wants to hear how talented you are... Your flesh wants to hear, "Can't nobody do it like you do." But Don't Believe the HYPE!

Many of you are purposed to become entrepreneurs, millionaires, men and women of great wealth and power, but God can't trust you to stay humble! You see, it's easy to be humble when you don't have anything... It's easy to be humble when you need help each month paying your bills... But can God trust you to stay humble when your "ship comes in"? Saints, you better get some people in your life like Daniel, who are willing to tell YOU the truth about YOU! We all want to be around people who pump us up and make us feel good about ourselves; but equally important are the people who keep it real! Get some people in your life that will tell you,

"Yes, you can cook, but there are people who can cook much better than you can!"

"Yes, you are a pretty girl, but you think you look better than you really do and you've got a bad attitude!"

"Yes, you give in the offering, but you're boastful about your giving..."

"Yes, you wear nice clothes, but you're arrogant and you think you're too cute to praise God..."

"Yes you're smart, but you think that you know it all and can't nobody tell you nothin' …"

"Yes you have a nice voice, but there's no anointing when you sing.'

'Yes you got a word from God, but there's too much flesh when you preach!"

Get somebody in your life who will tell you when you're wrong! Somebody who will tell you that you're selfish… Somebody who will tell you that you're mean and evil… Somebody who will tell you that you shouldn't be coveting that woman's husband…

Listen, I realize that it hurts when people talk about us, but sometimes we can even learn from our enemies. Our enemies don't look at us through the eyes of love; they examine us with a critical eye and then pick out all of our faults, and place them on Front Street. Instead of dismissing your enemies and saying, "They're just jealous of me because I have more than they have," listen to what they have to say, examine YOU and if there be any truth found, cry, "Lord I'll die!" We must realize that pride is sin and God will not tolerate sin!

> "The fear of the LORD is to hate evil: pride, and
> arrogancy,"
> (Proverbs 8:13) "

> "A haughty look, a proud heart…are sin."
> (Proverbs 21:4)

Our text tells that, one night while the king was in bed, he had a dream that frightened him. This powerful king who was a vicious warrior, this man who had killed thousands, a man who had been a man of war from his youth and had looked death in the face many times and not flinched… this mighty man was terrorized by a dream.

And although the king's bedroom was well guarded and his bed was soft and plush, the Bible tells us,

"Nebuchadnezzar had no peace" because his own thoughts made him uneasy and the visions of his head, the creatures of his own imagination, troubled him. It's a dangerous thing to think that you don't need anybody and that you have made it this far by yourself.

When you leave God out of the equation, He has a way of getting all up in your head. God has a way of getting your attention. I don't care how many college degrees you have on the wall... I don't care how popular you are... I don't care how many connections you have... I don't care what kind of car you drive... God will not share His glory!

Nebuchadnezzar was so despondent that he summoned all the wise men of Babylon so that they could interpret his dream. These men had interpreted the king's dreams before in a manner that pleased the king. Whether their interpretations were right or wrong... whether they hit or missed...the king liked what the wise men had to say;

But this time, none of them could give him an answer. At this point, the king seeks Daniel's advice after the other wise men couldn't help him.

> 7 "Then came in the magicians, the astrologers, the Chaldeans, and the soothsayers: and I told the dream before them; but they did not make known unto me the interpretation thereof.
> 8 But at the last Daniel came in before me, whose name was Belteshazzar, according to the name of my god, and in whom is the spirit of the holy gods: and before him I told the dream, saying,
> 9 O Belteshazzar, master of the magicians, because I know that the spirit of the holy gods is in thee, and no secret troubleth thee, tell me

the visions of my dream that I have seen, and
the interpretation thereof."
Daniel 4:7-9

Now, isn't it something that the King asked for
Daniel's advice last? Let's review the story… In the first
chapter of Daniel the Bible says that "in all matters of
wisdom and understanding the king found Daniel to be
ten times better than all the wise men in his entire realm."

> **19** And the king communed with them; and
> among them all was found none like Daniel,
> Hananiah, Mishael, and Azariah: therefore
> stood they before the king.
> **20** And in all matters of wisdom and
> understanding, that the king enquired of them,
> he found them ten times better than all the
> magicians and astrologers that were in all his
> realm."
> Daniel 1:19-20

In the second chapter of Daniel, the king has a dream
that none of the wise men could interpret and he was so
outraged that he was threatening to kill them all until
Daniel spoke up and divinely revealed the dream to him.

> **5** "The king answered and said to the
> Chaldeans, The thing is gone from me: if ye will
> not make known unto me the dream, with the
> interpretation thereof, ye shall be cut in pieces,
> and your houses shall be made a dunghill."
> Daniel 2:5

In the third chapter of Daniel we see three Jewish
boys who refused to obey the king's idolatrous decree and
they were cast into the fiery furnace; and the Bible says
that "the fire had no power" And when Nebuchadnezzar
saw this, he blessed the God of Shadrach, Meshach, and
Abednego!

18 "…be it known unto thee, O king, that we will not serve thy gods, nor worship the golden image which thou hast set up.

19 Then was Nebuchadnezzar full of fury, and the form of his visage was changed against Shadrach, Meshach, and Abednego: therefore he spake, and commanded that they should heat the furnace one seven times more than it was wont to be heated.

20 And he commanded the most mighty men that were in his army to bind Shadrach, Meshach, and Abednego, and to cast them into the burning fiery furnace.

21 Then these men were bound in their coats, their hosen, and their hats, and their other garments, and were cast into the midst of the burning fiery furnace…

25 He answered and said, Lo, I see four men loose, walking in the midst of the fire, and they have no hurt; and the form of the fourth is like the Son of God.

26 Then Nebuchadnezzar came near to the mouth of the burning fiery furnace, and spake, and said, Shadrach, Meshach, and Abednego, ye servants of the most high God, come forth, and come hither. Then Shadrach, Meshach, and Abednego, came forth of the midst of the fire.

27 And the princes, governors, and captains, and the king's counsellors, being gathered together, saw these men, upon whose bodies **the fire had no power**, nor was an hair of their head singed, neither were their coats changed, nor the smell of fire had passed on them.

28 Then Nebuchadnezzar spake, and said, Blessed be the God of Shadrach, Meshach, and Abednego, who hath sent his angel, and delivered his servants

that trusted in him, and have changed the
king's word, and yielded their bodies, that they
might not serve nor worship any god, except
their own God.
29 Therefore I make a decree, That every
people, nation, and language, which speak any
thing amiss against the God of Shadrach,
Meshach, and Abednego, shall be cut in pieces,
and their houses shall be made a dunghill:
because *there is no other God that can deliver*
after this sort."
Daniel 3:18-21 & 25-29

Although God continuously worked miracles
through His people, and even though God had proven
Himself time after time after time, we get to the forth
chapter and the king calls everyone but Daniel (a child of
God) for advice. Only when no one else could help him
did the king call Daniel. Why, after God had proven
Himself so many times before, did Nebuchadnezzar not
seek Daniel's revelation first?

It's the same old story. We know the answer to our
problems is in the Word of God, but we would rather call
our friends and see what they have to say. We know that
if we just lay on our face before God, HE will direct our
paths, but it's easier to sit in front of the TV and wish our
problems away. The old song says, "When you've tried
everything and everything has failed... try Jesus!" The
devil is a liar – try God first and then you won't need to
try everything!

God has spoken some things over your life, but in
some cases He's holding it back because He can't trust you
with it! He can't trust you with a better job because you
won't tithe off of the job that you have. He can't trust you
with a new car because you won't offer anyone a ride in
your old one. He can't bless you with a big house, because
you won't even keep your small apartment clean. God

can't bless you because you'll get high-minded and begin to look down at others.

God is waiting for you to kill pride so that He can trust you with His blessings! He wants to usher you into your destiny, but first your flesh must DIE! DIE until you refuse to take God's glory... DIE until it doesn't matter what people say about you... DIE until you uproot bitterness... DIE until you kill pride... DIE until you forget your childhood hurt... DIE until you love your enemies... DIE until the anointing comes... DIE so you can reach your family... DIE so you can reach your community... DIE so you can reach the nations... God can't use you until you DIE! You must mortify the deeds of your body.

> **12** "Therefore, brethren, we are debtors —
> not to the flesh, to live according to the flesh.
> **13** For if you live according to the flesh
> you will die; but if by the Spirit you put to
> death the deeds of the body, you will live.
> **14** For as many as are led by the Spirit
> of God, these are sons of God."
> Romans 8:13

> **28** "For it is in Him that we live, and move,
> and have our being;"
> Acts 17:28

Someone once said that your attitude determines your altitude, but God is saying today that your Humility determines your Destiny!

> **14** "If my people, which are called by my name,
> shall humble themselves, and pray, and seek
> my
> face, and turn from their wicked ways; then
> will I hear from heaven, and will forgive
> their sin, and will heal their land."
> 2Chronicles 7:14

God's ways are not our ways. In the order of God the path that leads up is down... the way to receive is to give... in order to live, you must die... the way to get ahead is by stepping back. Lowliness of mind and a readiness to prefer others before yourselves; gentleness, forgiveness of injuries; not quick to push forward your own interest – these are qualities that follow individuals who are led by the Spirit of God. Daniel remained humble and would not take God's glory...

> **46** "Then the king Nebuchadnezzar fell upon
> his face, and worshipped Daniel..."
> Daniel 2:46

Daniel refused to allow the King to infect him with the demonic spirit of pride; Daniel gave all the glory back to God! Although the King made Daniel ruler over the whole province of Babylon and made him the chancellor of the university and the chief of the governors over all the wise men of Babylon, Daniel never ceased to give God all the glory.

King Nebuchadnezzar ruled the most powerful empire the world had ever seen; but, until he honored God and gave Him the adoration and praise He deserved, Nebuchadnezzar became like an animal and crawled around on the ground like a dog. God wants to take us higher, to the next dimension in Him, but He is waiting for us to humble ourselves. Forget a title; labor in secret. Don't try to be up front; find whatever your hands can do in the Kingdom and work. Forget who gets the credit; God sees and He will reward you openly for what you do in secret.

> "That your charitable deed may be in secret;
> and your Father who sees in secret will
> Himself reward you openly."
> Matthew 6:4

In these last days you must seek His Deity above your dignity! Seek the Face of God. Seek the Presence of God. Seek the Heart of God. Seek the Righteousness of God. Get hungry for more of God... Get desperate for more of God...

> "Blessed are those who hunger and thirst for
> righteousness, For they shall be filled."
> Matthew 5:6

God is looking for a few people who will urgently, desperately chase Him. A select few who aren't concerned about the way they look or what others think about them – they just want to know more of God! God is searching for people who desire greater anointing and greater POWER... people who can lay hands on the sick and cancer dries up... people who can rebuke demons and they flee... people who pack supernatural, wonder-working POWER!

Chapter Seven

Travailing Sound

"Be in pain, and labour to bring forth,
O daughter of Zion, like a woman
in travail: for now shalt thou go
forth out of the city, and thou
shalt dwell in the field, and thou
shalt go even to Babylon; there
shalt thou be delivered; there the
LORD shall redeem thee from
the hand of thine enemies."
Micah 4:10

When we explore the meaning of TRAVAIL, we see that it is an action word. The American Heritage Dictionary defines travail as "The use of one's energy to do something: A difficult or tedious undertaking: The act or process of bringing forth...to work continually, especially with strenuous effort." So we see that to travail is not an easy task; it requires a great deal of energy and persistence and consistency in order to bring forth.

Throughout scripture we see that God operates through and responds to sound. Sound is the vehicle which transports our emotions, our desires, and our inner feelings from the spirit realm into the earth realm.

When Serena Williams hits the tennis ball, she makes a loud grunt... When asked why she makes this loud noise, she said that it enables her to hit the ball with greater force and precision. When professional fighters box, they often grunt and make noises as they throw and receive punches. These sounds depict anger and pain.

When a woman is in trouble, she'll scream in order to scare off the attacker and alert someone to help. Even on the most basic level, babies learn very early in life how to transport their feelings from their spirit realm into the earth realm. Babies know how to whine when their little spirits are lonely and they want to be picked up. When their spirits are scared of the dark, they know how to cry so that the light can be turned on. They instinctively know to scream when their spirits are angry in an attempt to have their own way.

Yes, children know how to use sound to get the immediate attention they desire; and even if you know there's nothing wrong with your child, most mothers when they hear their baby's cry, will instinctively go and check on the child just to make sure that everything is all right.

When the mother is certain everything is OK, she will often allow the child to continue crying. Although the sound is annoying, she realizes some crying is good for the child. Crying strengthens the child's lungs. Crying can help develop the child's vocal cords. Crying keeps the child from becoming spoiled, because the child will eventually learn to cry only when something is really wrong.

As a travailing Christian, don't ever think that God doesn't hear your cry. God hears your cry. He feels your pain. He knows your struggle. He counts your tears… And it is all a part of His perfecting process.

"…For it must needs be that offences come…"
Matthew 18:7

"…But your Father knoweth what things ye have
need of, before ye ask him"
Matthew 6:8

"….and weeping may endure for a night,
but joy cometh in the morning"
Psalms 30:5

Have you ever cried all night long? You desperately wanted to sleep, but even though your eyes were closed, your mind refused to slow down. Have you ever cried so long and so hard that there were no tears left to cry… all you could do was moan and groan? Well, take courage, my friend… God understands, even when you don't have a clue; and after all the hell you've been through, you've got some SERIOUS JOY coming!

"…the Spirit itself maketh intercession for us
with
groanings which cannot be uttered."
Roman 8:26

"They that sow in tears shall reap in joy"
Psalms 126:5

Sound is a channel by which the invisible is made visible. There's a Sound that causes things in the spirit realm to be manifested in the natural realm. There's a sound that causes miracles to take place. There's a sound that opens closed doors.

There is a sound that will break down strong holds; there's a sound that will tear down walls. You must understand that whatever you need, there is a sound that will usher it into your presence!

The ultimate desire of every believer should be a closer relationship with God. A sincere Christian craves an intimate, personal relationship with his Savior. David expressed it like this:

"As the deer pants for the water brooks,
So pants my soul for You, O God."

Psalms 42:1

There's a burning desire to be fully acquainted with God's Divine nature, with His character, His work and His salvation. There's an ever present longing to dwell with God, walk with God, live with God, to know His voice... to commune with God, to have Him breathe on you, to have Him rest on you. The song writer penned it so aptly when he said:

"To be like Jesus,
To be like Jesus,
On earth I long to be like Him...
All through life's journey,
From earth to glory,
I only ask,
I only ask,
To be like Him!"

Some people may be travailing for houses, cars, land, fur coats, fine jewelry, the riches of this world, BUT just give Me Jesus!

"One thing have I desired of the Lord, that
will I seek after; that I may dwell in the
house of the Lord all the days of my life,
to behold the beauty of the Lord, and
to enquire in his temple."
Psalms 27:4

Listen, there's nothing wrong with being prosperous and having nice things. God desires that His people have the best, but you will never truly enjoy the wealth of this world without putting God first! There is a formula to success and it is, "Seek ye first the kingdom of God and His righteousness; and then all these things shall be added." (Matthew 6:33)

Don't stoop to the world's madness... the greater One lives inside of you... You are who God says you are...

You can do what God says you can do... And you can have what God says you can have. But you've got to learn to face down and travail because the devil is just *not* going to let you have anything!

From the very beginning, God had big plans for you... You were formed in the image of God and after His likeness. You were designed for greatness. You were given dominion over all the earth. You were created to be the head and not the tail. God blessed you... He approved you... He loves you!

When we realize who we are in Christ Jesus and when we become as one... One in the spirit, One in Praise, One in worship... when we get on One Accord, One Mind, One Goal, One Mission... God said He would fill the house with His glory. Scripture supports the fact that God operates through sound. Just as He did on the day of Pentecost:

> "When the Day of Pentecost had fully come,
> they were all with one accord in one place."
> 2 And suddenly there came a sound from
> heaven, as of a rushing mighty wind, and it
> filled the whole house where they were sitting."
> Acts 2:1-2

When you're really in tune with God, you will hear the sound before you will ever see the manifestation. Just like on the day of Pentecost. First there was a sound, then the sound got louder and more intense until it filled the house, then the tongues appeared. Next, they were filled with the Holy Ghost, and then they spoke. But, before they ever received the gift, there was a sound! These vibrant sensations were accompanied by the majestic sound of at least 120 people worshiping and praising God! Yes... God operates through sound!!!

God has even gifted certain animals to be able to tap into the realm of sound. Elephants are so sensitive to sound that every one of them sensed the Tsunami long before it happened and, because they instinctively knew danger was approaching, the elephants fled to safety. I'm told that not one elephant died in the volcanic eruption because they heard it coming long before the native people ever had a clue of what was about to hit them! And because the natives couldn't tap into that realm of sound... tens of thousands of human lives were lost!

The emergency siren is designed to alert us to an emergency. When an ambulance is approaching, you hear the siren before you ever see the vehicle... and the closer the ambulance gets, the louder the siren becomes. The closer and the louder the siren gets, it's designed to drown out other noises so that all you hear is the SIREN!

My husband and I have some close friends who lost their son in a terrible automobile accident. He was driving his car while playing loud music and his windows were all up, so he couldn't hear the fire truck's siren. The truck crashed into him at an intersection and he died instantly. He had not positioned himself to hear the sound that could have saved his life!

Listen, there are setups, tragedies, pitfalls, things the devil has planned with your name on them, that you can actually arrest in the spirit realm and prevent them from ever taking place here on earth. But this will only happen when you position yourself to hear the sound.

Salvation is FREE, but the anointing will cost you something. Roll down the window of carnality, turn off the radio of gossip, get on your face in prayer, and get in the Word of God so that you can hear the sound! Don't wait until trouble comes to your address, to start seeking God's voice. You've got to continually get in God's presence so that you can be sensitive to His sound.

God's sound drowns out the devil. God's sound drowns out confusion and mess. God's sound can abort tragedies. God's voice unfolds mysteries. His voice reveals signs and wonders. God's voice reveals your purpose. God's voice unfolds your destiny. YES... There is a Sound!

In scripture, when the Jewish people blew the Shofar, one of the things that it signified was that war was about to take place! The sound of the horn let all of the people far and near know to prepare themselves for battle! We too must prepare for battle because we are at WAR!

"...the kingdom of heaven suffereth violence,
and the violent take it by force."
Matthew 11:12

Life isn't a game; the devil is not playing with us. The devil doesn't know everything that God has waiting for you, but he knows enough about God to know that whatever God has for His children is some GREAT STUFF! I don't know about you, but when I enter into worship, I'm not trying to look cute. Tears might roll down my face, my nose might be runny, my hair might mess up, I might catch a run in my stockings, but I'm desperate for more of God and I'm desperate for ALL of my STUFF!

There's a song that says, "Give Me My Stuff Back," but I don't just want my old stuff back... I also want my stuff that I haven't even seen yet! There's some stuff that I know God has for me... and I want it ALL!

You've suffered long enough... take your stuff back by force!

In Biblical history, the sound of the Shofar also represented the presence of God! When the Israelites heard the horn, they would shout so powerfully, that the very sound intimidated their enemy. When the enemy heard the sound, they feared because it reminded them of the God of Israel and how God fought for the Jews, causing them to miraculously win their battles.

"And when the ark of the covenant of the
LORD
came into the camp, all Israel shouted with a
great
shout, so that the earth rang again. And when
the
Philistines heard the noise of the shout, they
understood that the ark of the LORD
was come into the camp."
1Samuel 4:5-6

Even when the Israelites were up against armies that were greater in number and strength, and greater in knowledge and technology, God would step in and fight for them. God would cause an earthquake, a storm or a mud slide to overtake the enemy. He would cause the earth's elements to fight for His people! When you saturate the atmosphere with the right sound, you won't need a hookup. With the right sound you won't need a connection. With the right sound you won't need somebody to give you a break.

Everyone may be against you… the odds may not be in your favor… others may be smarter than you… they may have more experience than you; but when you make the right sound, you tap into a ZONE that transports you straight into the Supernatural, where you don't need any mortal's help. Even when people have their feet on you, God will supernaturally raise you up ABOVE those around you and there won't be anything they can do about it because when God blesses you… You're JUST Blessed!

"Now it shall come to pass, if you diligently
obey the voice of the LORD your God, to
observe carefully all His commandments
which I command you today, that the
LORD your God will set you high

above all nations of the earth."
Deuteronomy 28:1

You see, man's blessings are for a season, but God's blessings are eternal. You don't need anybody's help getting what God has for you. Just tap into the sound that will get God's attention! Tap into the sound that will intimidate the devil into releasing your stuff! A lot of you are pregnant with potential and possibility, you're pregnant with dreams, pregnant with ministry, pregnant with business ideas, pregnant with CREATIVTY, pregnant with greatness – and God is saying, "It's time to give birth!"

I heard a preacher say, "The devil has attacked the REPRODUCTIVE SYSTEM of the church." Christians start out in various areas of ministry, but as time goes by, you look up and their assignments are aborted! They may sing in the choir for a while, then they quit. They may be on the usher board for a while, then they quit. They may work with the outreach team for a while, then they quit. They go to one church for a while, but when opposition hits, they leave and go to another church. They never stick with anything long enough to give birth to their purposed destiny. When things get rough, they run for the border! The devil has attacked their reproductive systems!

We must understand that some things come to us easier than others. My children were all gifts from God, but some of them came easier than others. The birthing process for one of my children was a Struggle! With most of my children I was only in labor for a few hours, but there was one child who just refused to come. My water had broken, the baby's head had crowned, he was in position, but I labored for twenty-four hours before he was born.

The doctors were saying that both the baby and my vitals were dropping and that if he didn't deliver soon, they would have to take my child through an emergency C-section.   At that point, I prayed and I pushed and I yelled with all of my strength, and my son came forth!

YES... I was tired... I was drained... I was at my wits' end. But I refused to give up because I was on the brink of something wonderful! I had come too far to have them take something on which I had worked so hard to bring forth naturally. When I made up my mind that I was going to have that baby naturally, God gave me an inner strength that amazed even me, and shortly thereafter my ten-pound Devon was born!

We must understand that some gifts and talents we were born with. We didn't have to pray them into manifestation; we didn't have to work for them; we didn't have to sweat for them; they were already with us... They came easy. But don't fool yourself... There are some things that you're going to have to fight for! There are things that God has stored up for you in the spirit realm that you will never receive until you learn how to call them forth into manifestation!

> "Let them shout for joy, and be glad, that
> favour my righteous cause: yea, let them say
> continually, Let the LORD be magnified,
> which hath pleasure in the prosperity of his
> servant."
> Psalm 35:27

Listen, God wants to see you prosper, but you are going to have to O p e n – Y o u r – M o u t h! We don't serve no little, quiet statue who sits up on a shelf... We serve the ALMIGHTY GOD, THE CREATOR OF THE UNIVERSE... A GOD OF SOUND!

> "For the Lord himself shall descend from
> heaven with a shout, with the voice of the
> archangel, and with the trump of God: and the
> dead in Christ shall rise first:"

1Thessalonians 4:16

When the Lord comes back, He's not sneaking in around the corner; He's coming back with a SHOUT that's Packing POWER! POWER that will raise the dead, POWER that will rapture His saints from every nation and continent… POWER that will do all of this in the twinkling of an eye! And your Bible says that His POWER will come With – A - SHOUT!

They used to call us the Holy Rollers and the Noisy Bunch because the church of old knew how to get God's attention. But now – we are getting so sophisticated with our worship that our shout has to be cute and our dance has to be choreographed. God is telling us to go back to the days of old, so we can see what the old-timers saw and do what our forefathers did. God has not changed… He's the same today, yesterday and forever!

We're the ones who have changed and it's time to go back! If GOD used Mother Boyd to raise the dead, I want that same power! If He used Mother Pool to raise people out of wheel chairs, I want that same power! If He used Smith Wigglesworth to raise the dead and give sight to the blind, I want that same power! If He used G. T. Haywood to birth an international organization of tongues-talking believers, both black and white, at a time when racism was at its peak, I want that same power!

Aren't you sick of being average? Is anybody tired of being mediocre? Then press for more and don't settle for less! If you're really desperate for a move of God… if you're sick and tired of being sick and tired… if you're tired of church as usual…. if you're at the point where you really don't care what people think about you… if you could care less what people are saying about you…. then you're on the brink of your Breakthrough! All you've got to do is tap into the sound that will dispatch change!

"And Elijah said unto Ahab, Get thee up, eat
and drink; for there is a sound of abundance of
rain."
1Kings 18:41

Get Up... for there's a sound of abundance in your house! Stop living in Lack...

Stop operating in Defeat.... Stop allowing FEAR to hold you hostage...

Don't miss your Blessing... Don't miss your Miracle... Don't miss your Season....

Listen... Listen... Listen... There's a sound of abundance in the house!

"Blow ye the trumpet in Zion, and sound an
alarm
in my holy mountain: let all the inhabitants of
the
land tremble: for the day of the LORD cometh,
for it is nigh at hand;"
Joel 2:1

The Lord is coming soon. His coming is closer now than ever before. Jesus could come back literally at any moment.

"So the people shouted when the priests blew
with
 the trumpets: and it came to pass, when the
people heard the sound of the trumpet, and the
people shouted with a great shout, that the
wall fell down flat, so that the people went
up into the city, every man straight
before him, and they took the city."
Joshua 6:20

When we tap into the right sound, we will shake hell and make a difference in our communities. It's time for us to stop letting the devil wreak havoc in our families, in our finances, and even in our bodies. We must learn to prepare the atmosphere for Miracles... Prepare this place For Healing... Prepare for the Holy Ghost to Fall Fresh... Usher in God's Presence! Prepare for the Glory Cloud to appear! Prepare your heart to receive! Whatever you need from the Lord, it's already here, and we've just got to prepare to receive it! And your preparation is in your SOUND!

God commands us, to MAKE A SOUND!

"O clap your hands, all ye people; shout unto
God with the voice of triumph."
Psalms 47:1

"Make a joyful noise unto the LORD, all the
earth:
make a loud noise, and rejoice, and sing
praise."
Psalms 98:4

YOUR MIRACLE IS IN YOUR SOUND! The world thinks we're crazy when we shout and make noise in church... they think we're foolish.

"...God hath chosen the foolish things of
the world to confound the wise..."
1Corinthians 1:27

So, if you want to confuse your enemy... If you want to get him off track, tap into the sound, the sound that will loose shackles... the sound that will break chains... the sound that will heal the sick... the sound that will bind demons... the sound that will dispatch angels. I'm not talking about a wimpy sound, I'm not talking about a faint sound, I'm not talking about a weak or pitiful sound... I'm talking about a victorious sound... a sound that demands attention, a sound that alerts heaven, a sound that shakes hell, a sound that transcends nations and nationalities... A sound that confuses the Devil.

Yes, there is a sound and it's the sound of Worship...
It's the sound of PRAISE! It's the midnight hour, and
today God is going to open some doors and loose some
bands. Lord, we summon your power. Oh God, show us
your strength, oh God, as you have done before. You are
awesome, oh God! Give power and strength to your
people!!! We prepare the atmosphere for Your presence,
mighty God!!!!!

Chapter Eight

Positioned to Hear

"Incline your ear, and come unto me: hear, and
your soul shall live; and I will make an
everlasting covenant with you, even the sure
mercies of David."
Isaiah 55:3

I submit to you that everything in the universe has
an ear. An *ear* is defined as, *"Responsiveness to the sounds or
forms of spoken language:"* I further suggest that everything
in the universe can hear, for to *hear* is *"To perceive and pay
attention to."* The Word of God reveals that during creation
God spoke to the light and there was light. God told the
earth to bring forth grass and trees and it was so.
Scripture indicates that even mountains can hear.

"And he (Jesus) arose, and rebuked the wind,
and
said unto the sea, Peace, be still. And the wind
ceased, and there was a great calm."
Mark 4:39

"…for verily I say unto you, If ye have faith as a
grain of mustard seed, ye shall say unto this
mountain, remove hence to yonder place; and it
shall remove; and nothing shall be impossible
unto you"
Matthew 17:20

Yes, all of creation can hear and when God speaks,
all of creation listens! You may not understand, you may
not be ready to receive, you may even choose to ignore,
but when God speaks, you will hear! The question is will

you obey? We see in the first few chapters of Mark, Jesus speaks; He's preaching the Word, teaching in parables, casting out demons, performing miracles; He's appointing disciples and endowing them with power. He's defining and defending the gospel and He's even rebuking and condemning unbelievers.

Jesus was also confronting Sabbath controversies. As you may know, the observance of not working on the Sabbath day had become a legalistic obligation and the Pharisees condemned anyone who worked on the Sabbath. The Bible says that the Pharisees watched Jesus closely so they could accuse Him. They spied on Him, if you will. They weren't following Him to get greater knowledge and understanding... they weren't concerned about seeing people healed, delivered and set free... they weren't concerned about hearing God... all the Pharisees wanted to do was to closely examine Jesus' every word in order to find fault and ultimately destroy Him.

The same is true today: we've got some spies in the church! Everyone who comes to church is not coming to get closer to God. Some people come to church simply to see what's going on and to find fault! They don't want to do any better, they're not trying to hear a word from God, they're not trying to be loosed and delivered, they're not trying to see you loosed and delivered either: They're on an assignment straight from hell to discredit and destroy the ministry! That's why when we come into the house of the Lord, we've got to saturate the temple with the Holy Ghost, we've got to invoke the presence of the almighty God and we've got to stop making it so easy for the devil to get in.

How often have you thought, "There's such a heaviness on the service... Are we going to be able to break through?" Listen, child of God, you are not a wimp! You've got the power to block Satan's assignment because the Greater One lives inside you! But you must position yourself to hear God. Consider the following scriptures:

"Hearken; Behold, there went out a sower to sow:

4 And it came to pass, as he sowed, some fell by the way side, and the fowls of the air came and devoured it up.

5 And some fell on stony ground, where it had not much earth; and immediately it sprang up, because it had no depth of earth:

6 But when the sun was up, it was scorched; and because it had no root, it withered away.

7 And some fell among thorns, and the thorns grew up, and choked it, and it yielded no fruit.

8 And other fell on good ground, and did yield fruit that sprang up and increased; and brought forth, some thirty, and some sixty, and some an hundred.

9 And he said unto them, He that hath ears to hear, let him hear"

Mark 4:3-9

We see that on the Sabbath Jesus goes out with the disciples into the grain fields and on purpose they pluck the heads of grain. We see Jesus deliberately heal a man with a withered hand on the Sabbath. And the Bible says that when the Pharisees saw this, they immediately plotted to destroy Jesus.

We must understand that there are those in the church today who are literally stuck in the past... they are held hostage to legalism and tradition. God is moving in a mighty way, but because things aren't being done as they were twenty-five years ago, they say it's not God. To anyone who is stuck in the past, these next few sentences are for you:

The message must not change, but the method may have to! God may call the man or woman of God to do things a little differently, but because we are so bound to tradition and legalism and the way we used to do things, we miss what God is trying to accomplish through us. God may call us to take our prayer warriors into a night club one Friday night and radically infiltrate the club with the Word of God, but because we were taught back in the days of old that it was a sin to go into a night club, you talk against the vision.

God may call us into the crack houses to snatch out the drug addicts, but, because back in the "good ol' days" you were taught that the sinner needed to come to church in order to get saved, you discredit the vision. God may send you out on the street corner to rescue the prostitute, but you won't go because you're scared that someone might see you. WAKE UP CHURCH! We are living in the last days and God has commissioned us to go out and get the lost!

> "And the lord said unto the servant, Go out into
> the
> highways and hedges, and compel them to
> come in,
> that my house may be filled"
> Luke 14:23

People are hungry for Truth and we've got to be willing to share the gospel by any means necessary! We've got to go beyond just barely being able to stay saved from week to week. God can't trust you to go into a club and witness when you were in the club the night before getting your groove on. God can't send you into the crack house when you're dealing drugs on the side yourself. You can't tell anybody that God can deliver them from alcohol when you are still sipping gin. God is

calling His people to be the real deal... because even the
devil knows if you're a fake!

The scripture tells us that great multitudes followed
Jesus as He performed miracles and even the unclean
spirits, when they saw Jesus, fell down before Him crying
out, *"You are the son of God."* You can fool the people some
of the time, but you can't fool God and you can't even fool
the devil. Consider the following scripture:

"And the evil spirit answered and said, Jesus I
know,
and Paul I know; but who are ye?
And the man in whom the evil spirit was
leaped on them, and overcame them, and
prevailed against them, so that they fled out of
that
house naked and wounded"
Acts 19:15-16

It's a dangerous thing to pretend to operate in the
anointing of God. The devil will jump on you, call you
out, embarrass you, put you on Front Street and make you
look like an utter fool! When you are truly anointed of
God, when you are earnestly and sincerely walking with
God, when you desperately pursue a personal relationship
with God, every demon in hell knows you by name. They
are scared to death of you because you carry the name of
Jesus! At the name of Jesus demons tremble and flee. You
may not have tapped into it yet, but even the devil knows
there's POWER IN THE NAME OF JESUS! Consider the
following scriptures:

"Wherefore God also hath highly exalted him,
and given him a name which is above every
name:
That at the name of Jesus every knee should
bow, of things in heaven, and things in earth,
and things under the earth; And that every

tongue should confess that Jesus Christ is Lord,
to the glory of God the Father"
Philippians 2:9-11

You don't have to fake it, just take on the name of
Jesus and you'll receive POWER!

"But ye shall receive power, after that the
Holy Ghost is come upon you:"
Acts 1:8

The Bible says that the scribes saw the power of Jesus
and they said, "He has Beelzebub and by the ruler of the
demons he casts our demons."

JESUS RESPONDED BY SAYING,

"And if a kingdom be divided against itself,
that kingdom cannot stand. And if a house be
divided against itself, that house cannot stand.
And if Satan rise up against himself, and be
divided, he cannot stand, but hath an end"
(Mark 3:24-26).

Read this carefully: You will never find a more
unified group than Satan and his imps and demons. You
will never read in the Bible where demons are fighting
against each other. The enemy has one common goal and
it's to KILL, STEAL and to DESTROY and he is working
overtime all over the world trying to accomplish his
mission. Satan has a well-organized, well-unified regime
that carries out his orders... and one of his main strategies
is to make sure that the people of God never become
united! The devil wants to keep us arguing about
doctrine, fussing about clothes and jewelry, pointing our
fingers at each other, talking about each other, fighting
and killing each other because he knows that if we ever
truly become bonded together in love, we will WHIP HIM
TO A FRAZZLE AND SEND HIM AND HIS DEMONS
STRAIGHT BACK TO HELL WITH THEIR TAILS

BETWEEN THEIR LEGS! We must learn to work together!

Further in the text we see that God declared that, because the scribes blasphemed against the Holy Ghost and said that Jesus was of the devil, they would never be forgiven of their sins and they would be subject to eternal condemnation. Here the Word admonishes you to watch what you say about the people of God; be careful how you treat God's anointed; don't poke fun at the Holy Spirit and don't nitpick and try to discredit the Word of God. Don't be so quick to criticize and say who's of God and who isn't. Don't be so quick to judge who's saved and who isn't.

Be careful because when God writes you off, it's over! One of the reasons Jesus spoke in parables was to conceal the truth from those who had rejected Him. Yes, parables enlightened those who sought the truth, but they also blinded the disobedient. Consider the following scripture:

> "And he said unto them, Unto you it is given to know the mystery of the kingdom of God: but unto them that are without, all these things are done in parables: That seeing they may see, and not perceive; and hearing they may hear, and not understand; lest at any time they should be converted, and their sins should be forgiven them."
> Mark 4:11-12

Don't play with God; He will fix it so you will hear the Word and not be able to receive it. It's time out for playing games with the adversary. We must get busy about our Father's business. If you are a blood-bought, born-again Christian, you are a disciple of Christ and you have been commissioned to tell every creature with whom you come in contact about our Lord and Savior Jesus

Christ! Therefore, anyone who proclaims the gospel is a sower of the Word. You may never preach behind a pulpit, you may never teach a Bible class or a Sunday school lesson, but you must share Jesus with the lost and dying world.

> "Now he that planteth and he that watereth are one:
> and every man shall receive his own reward according to his own labour"
> 1Corinthians 3:8

We must stop waiting on the pastor and the ministers of the church to preach sinners into the body of Christ... It's time to own up to our responsibility… one plants… one waters and God gives the increase. We're in this thing together!

If you want to know what your purpose is, if you want to know what it is that you were created to do, here's the answer: You were created to give God glory and to bring others to Christ! You will never live a life of fullness and contentment until you get busy about your Father's business.

Often we become discouraged when we tell people about Jesus and they don't seem to want to hear us. You invite friends and loved ones to church year after year and they never come. You pray for your co-workers when they are experiencing hard times, but they only want a quick fix for an immediate problem… they don't want the Problem Solver. You raise your children up in church, but when they grow up, they don't serve God…

Yes, being a disciple for Christ can be quite challenging. But we must understand that the effect of the preaching of the Word depends upon the state of the hearer's heart, not on you. In order to receive a Word from God, the recipient's heart must be positioned to hear.

In the fourth chapter of Mark, Jesus refers to various conditions of the ground being representative of the hearts of man:

1. Stony ground
2. Shallow ground
3. Weeded ground
4. Good ground.

1. The *stony ground* He likens to a hard heart. These individuals are bitter and have something against God. They attend church only by habit; they feel as though they are doing God a favor by going to church; they are constantly on the defensive and dare anyone to approach them or they vow to snap! They won't clap, sing, pray, give a dime in offering (although they will probably walk around for offering so they can show off their outfits).

The stony heart is very critical of everybody and everything. This person is constantly finding fault, has a great big chip on his shoulder and nothing that is being done in church, from the beginning to the end, touches him in any way. The Word of God has fallen on stony ground... it has fallen on a hard heart, a heart that was not positioned to hear. It's like bird seed sprinkled onto concrete: when you walk away from the seed, the birds will come and eat them up because they were spread on top of the ground. When your heart is hard and callous, the Word of God cannot penetrate your spirit and minister to your soul – it simply falls upon your hearing and as quickly as you hear it, the devil steels it from you.

Yes, you came to church; yes, you heard the message preached; yes, you heard the songs of Zion; yes, you heard the prayer of faith; yes, you watched the saints worship and praise God, but it was all in vain because your heart was stony and, as quickly as the Word fell upon your heart, the devil stole it.

"The thief cometh not, but for to steal, and to
kill, and to destroy: I am come that they might
have life, and that they might have it more
abundantly"
John 10:10

The Word of God is life, it is the only thing in this
world that can sustain you. If the devil steals the Word
from you, he has stolen your life! Stop being so hard, just
let "IT" go! "It" might be a grudge; "It" might be an
abused childhood; "It" might be a bad marriage; "It"
might be that you can't find a job; "It" might be people
talking about you; "It" might be that you're broke, but
whatever "It" is, God is bigger and He came to save you
from "It." But He has to have a soft, receptive heart to rest
upon.

2.   The next type of ground that our scripture talks
about is *shallow ground*. Here we see a person who has
heard the Word and has allowed it to superficially
penetrate them. This saint lacks depth and substance. Let
me put it so you can better understand it: this saint is weak
as water. They're screaming and shouting on Sunday
morning, but by the time Sunday night rolls around,
somebody has made them mad and they're cussing like a
sailor. They're on FIRE for God on Sunday, but by
Monday when they go to work, no one can tell that they
even go to church. They're full of love on Sunday, but
mean as the devil's first cousin the rest of the week.
They're more concerned about what they are going to
wear to church than they are about preparing their hearts
for worship. This individual is not rooted and grounded
in the Word of God. He or she has no relationship with
God, but simply goes through the motions...

"Having a form of godliness, but denying the
power
thereof: from such turn away."

2Timothy 3:5

A true relationship with God does not come from your shout and your dance; singing in the choir won't draw you closer to God either. Being on the usher board won't give you the mind of Christ. Being a member of the dance ministry won't give you a heart for the things of God; serving on the Pastor's Aid won't enable you to hear the voice of God. In order to be positioned to hear God, you must be rooted and grounded in the Word of God; you must have a relationship with God.

3.   Then there's the *weeded ground*. This is when you've allowed the cares of life, the love of money, and other things to choke the Word out and you have become unfruitful. Weeds will take over if you let them. Weed roots go deep, you can't just cut a weed; you've got to pull weeds up by the root or they will grow right back and bring their relatives with them. Weeds multiply quickly when not dealt with. Weeds are nonproductive and they must go! Weeds don't bare any fruit... they are useless.

4.   Finally there's *good ground*. Ministers of every stripe, whether teacher, preacher, prophet, saint – even sinners – should aspire to be good ground. The scripture says that good ground will hear and accept the Word and bear fruit 30-, 60- and 100-fold.

> "Herein is my Father glorified, that ye bear much
> fruit; so shall ye be my disciples"
> John 15:8

We must bear the fruit of the spirit... Love, Joy, Peace, Longsuffering, Gentleness, Goodness, Faith.

> "Ye have not chosen me, but I have chosen you,
> and ordained you, that ye should go and bring
> forth fruit, and that your fruit should remain:

that whatsoever ye shall ask of the Father in my
name, he may give it you"
John 15:16

Do you want your needs met? Do you want to fulfill
your purpose? Are you tired of the devil taking over your
life? Then position yourself to hear from God.

Consider the following illustration: If I were to
attend a seminar and the facilitator was speaking French, I
would hear her, but, because I don't understand the
French language, I would not be able to receive what she
was saying. The class may be very informative and there
may be a wealth of knowledge to gain, but, because I don't
have the ability to understand French, I'm simply wasting
my time. In order to get anything out of a seminar taught
in French, I must either have an interpreter or, before
taking the class, I must learn the French language.

Now, French is not the easiest language to learn, so if
I took an hour of French class each week, it would take me
a lifetime to learn the language fluently. However, if I
lived in France for three or four years, with no English
speaking people to communicate with, I would be forced
to communicate in French and I would probably learn to
speak French more quickly.

What I'm trying to say is that some of you come to
church form Sunday to Sunday and you hear the Word of
God, but you don't receive what is being said because you
don't understand the things of God; they just don't make
much sense, it's foreign to you. You have ears but you
don't have ears to hear. It makes no sense to you when
you hear that saints are to turn the other cheek when
someone slaps them in the face... It makes no sense to
bless those who curse you; it makes no sense to love your
enemies; it makes no sense to declare healing when your
body is racked with pain; it makes no sense to pay tithes
and give offering when you have bills that are overdue.

But in order to really understand the things of God, you must take on the mind of Christ.

God's ways are far different from the ways of our flesh and you will never really know Him just by coming to church on Sundays. The only way to really take on the mind of Christ is by totally yielding to God. You must yield to an intimate prayer life... yield to denying your flesh and fasting... yield to keeping your bodies free from sin... yield to giving... yield to reading God's word... yield to working in the Kingdom... yield to witnessing... yield to bringing souls into the kingdom. Face down, position yourself to hear and then YIELD!

Shortly after I committed to spending more time in prayer, I had a disagreement with someone who knew that my prayer time had increased tremendously. During the somewhat heated conversation, this person referred to me as, "Miss Prayer Warrior." The implication was that all of my praying was not doing me any good.

Although my spirit was grieved and my anger kindled, I didn't respond to the comment. I began to wonder if what had been implied was true. Then the Lord ministered to my spirit and let me know that this was just a trick of the adversary (devil) to discourage me from pressing into prayer.

Just because you are not perfected overnight, don't allow the enemy to cause you to think that a lifestyle of prayer is ineffective. Please face down and keep praying! There are two things that will happen if you continue in prayer: First, you will not get any worse. The situation may appear more intense, but trust God, it's working for your good. Second, you will not remain the same. Whether you realize it or not, God is perfecting you. He is digging deep within your spirit and surfacing all of your impurities so that He can cleanse you from all unrighteousness.

Don't give up on prayer. Without prayer, you have no life support and death is inevitable! Now, to the person who tries to intimidate, taunt and judge those who pray, be careful. When you decide to go deep there are those who will despise the anointing that is on your life. Scripture tells us that when King Saul saw the spirit of God on David, he was jealous and he was overcome with a bitter hatred toward David and on many occasions sought to kill him. There are those who will hate you because of your anointing. They will seek to destroy you with their tongues. But if God be for you, it's more than the world against you!

> "When the wicked, even mine enemies and my
> foes,
> came upon me to eat up my flesh, they
> stumbled and fell."
> Psalms 27:2

The more the enemy oppresses you, the more God will raise you up! You will be like David: the more Saul sought to destroy David; the more endeared he became to the people, especially Jonathan, Saul's son, and the more David prospered exceedingly. Draw near to God and He will draw near to you!

Chapter Nine

In Desperate Pursuit

'That I may know him, and the power of his
resurrection, and the fellowship of his
sufferings, being made conformable unto his
death;"
Philippians 3:10

"Acquaint now thyself with him, and be at
peace:
thereby good shall come unto thee."
Job 22:21

One of the greatest desires of a Christian is to know
Christ. Not just to have heard about Him, or to have read
about Him, but to really know Him.

We are often intrigued as we read about the lives of
many of the famous movie stars and secular singers that
appear in the newspaper headlines. Michael Jackson has
been in the spotlight just about all of his life. We've
watched him grow up; we've seen him move from a small
house in Gary, Indiana to a mansion in Beverly Hills,
California. We've watched as he went from poverty status
to   obtaining   millions   of   dollars.
We've seen his dramatic physical transformation from
dark skin, to light skin, from short, nappy hair to a jerry
curl, and then to long straight hair. We have watched his
face transfigure from a wide, pug nose, to a long, thin
nose… from a round, smooth chin to a dimpled, pointed
chin. We have seen Michael change from an innocent
child to an accused child molester. But, with all that we

have seen and heard about the "star" Michael Jackson, most people don't know who he really is.

Consider the people in your family. How well do you know your spouse? How reliable are your predictions regarding your children, your friends, and your loved-ones? Let's get really personal: how well do you really know yourself? Have you ever had a thought cross your mind that was totally out of your character... something so shocking that all you could do is wonder where in the world did that come from? Have you ever reacted to a situation in a way that you thought you never would because you were certain that the Lord had delivered you from that type of behavior? Well, regardless of how well you think you know yourself, or how saved you think you are, the Bible lets us know that God is the only one who knows your heart.

> "For the LORD searcheth all hearts, and
> understandeth all the imaginations of
> the thoughts: if thou seek him, he will
> be found of thee; but if thou forsake
> him, he will cast thee off for ever."
> 1Chronicles 28:9

People seek to associate with those whom they feel are important. Groupies and *wannabees* will go to great lengths to be around the popular crowd. They'll buy clothes they can't afford, cars and houses they can't maintain, all in an attempt to "keep up with the Joneses." They define their self-worth by their worldly possessions and by the stuff they have acquired. All of their attention is placed on the outer man. They work overtime on their jobs just to keep their hair and nails done, to wear clothes with the right name in the label, to carry designer bags, to wear Jordan tennis shoes and to keep up with the latest fads.

While all of this attention is placed on temporal possessions, their insides are a mess. They've become so engrossed with the things of this world that they have neglected their spirit man.

"For what shall it profit a man, if he shall gain the
whole world, and lose his own soul?"
Mark 8:36

The truth is, most of us will never hobnob with the rich and famous and the stars of this world may never know our names. You may not be invited to their parties, or offered membership in their high-class clubs... but there is a star who wants to get acquainted with you...

"I Jesus have sent mine angel to testify unto you these things in the churches. I am the root and the offspring of David, and the bright and morning star."
Revelation 22:16

Yes, He is the mega star who desires an up-close and personal relationship with you, and His name is Jesus! The fact is that no other person has impacted this world like the Lord Jesus Christ! Whether you accept or reject Him, acknowledge or ignore Him, receive or deny Him, He's the STAR! I take my hat off to President Barrack Obama, Oprah Winfrey, Stevie Wonder, and Denzel Washington, who have all made tremendous strides in their respective fields, but if I never get the opportunity to meet any of them, just give me JESUS!

When you desperately pursue Jesus you don't have time for the cliques... you don't trip out because you weren't invited to dinner... you don't get upset when people don't speak to you... you're not trying to get invited to all of the barbeques... you don't need people to validate you because you know who you are in Christ Jesus! You are the King's kid! You're an heir and a joint heir with Christ Jesus. You have a rich inheritance coming that man has absolutely nothing to do with; so why try so hard to please each other and forget about pleasing God?

Stop working so hard to get man's approval. People will love you today and crucify you tomorrow. They'll build you up, just to let you down. They'll smile in your face and stab you in your back. They'll be with you today and they won't even know who you are tomorrow. But if you would just get desperate for Jesus, He will never leave you nor forsake you. He's the same yesterday, today and forever. He's a friend that sticks closer than a brother, and if God be for you, He's more than the world against you.

If God be for you, you won't have to politic your way in, you don't have to buy your way in, you won't have to be voted in. As a matter of fact, you will look back and thank those who shut you out because it drove you to your knees, it drove you face down, closer to God!

Travel with me back to the book of beginnings, where we will examine with spiritual insight the character and the nature of God. As you study the first chapter, you'll see the God of all creation in His renowned power, displaying His awesome greatness. In Genesis, God creates and then He surveys each new creation – day, Earth and seas, vegetation, lights in the firmament of the heavens, living creatures of the sea and air, living land creatures... and daily, with a fresh thrill of joy, He pronounces... "Good!"

But it's His climax of creation, Man, that causes God to boldly declare, "Very Good." Saints, from day one God had big plans for you! You were formed in the image of God and after His likeness. You were designed for greatness. You were given dominion over all of the earth. You were created to be the head and not the tail! He blessed you, He approved you because He loves you.

As we further explore the character and nature of God we see that

"In the beginning God created the heaven and the earth."
Genesis 1:1

Here we see that God is infinite, eternal, self existent and the cause of all that is. As Moses affirms,

"Before the mountains were brought forth, or ever
thou hadst formed the earth and the world, even
from everlasting to everlasting, thou art God."
Psalms 90:2

God is above, independent of, and prior to all that has been created in heaven and in earth.

"And the earth was without form, and void; and
darkness was upon the face of the deep. And the
Spirit of God moved upon the face of the waters."
Genesis 1:2

Here we see that God is a God of order for He brings order out of total chaos. Although the Bible doesn't describe in great detail exactly what the earth looked like prior to the above verse, we do know that the earth was a mess... in total disorder and confusion. Scholars point out that the word, "was," in this passage, could also be translated, "had become." So this scripture could also read, *the earth had become waste and empty."*

Since we know that God is not the author of waste and emptiness, we must conclude that the earth, in its original state, displayed perfection and order. Even Satan was created perfect, until iniquity was found in him.

But between verses one and two a great catastrophe occurred.   Something   terrible   happened   to   create confusion and disorder.   Something happened to cause God's original, perfect earth to become without form and void. Only a powerful disaster could explain the chaotic condition of verse 2.   Scripture tells us that because of Satan's arrogance and because he wanted to take God's place, he was cast down to the earth along with one third of the angelic host.

May I suggest to you that Satan and his posse fell onto the earth and this caused the earth, God's original perfect creation, to become without form and void? Wherever Satan and his demons are, chaos is present. Just think back to when Satan controlled your life; look back over your life of sin, think about where God found you, remember where God brought you from:

Some of you were petty thieves... alcoholics... drug addicts... drug pushers... prostitutes... liars... cheaters... murderers... backbiters... whoremongers... adulterers.... fornicators... hypocrites (church sinners – people who profess one thing in church, but live the total opposite). If I didn't mention your sin, you just fill in the blank! The bottom line is, when the devil had us, we were a total mess!!!! All too often we walk around with our nose in the air, as if we were born saved.   We don't want to acknowledge what we used to be, but in order for God to get the glory out of our lives, we must let the world know that God is greater than the devil! And if they ask how do you know? you tell them, "Just look at me!!! I'm a living witness that God will bring order out of your mess!"

Child of God, you may not be all that you want to be, but as you look over your past, you should be able to say... you're no way near what you used to be; God changed your walk, He changed your talk, He cleaned you up, He changed your desires. The places that you used to go to, you don't want to go there anymore; the things you used to do, you don't do any more; the things that used to give you pleasure, utterly disgust you now. That's because God brought order out of your chaos! Satan is the ruler of this world, so we shouldn't be surprised that the nations of this world are experiencing massive turmoil… wars, earthquakes, hurricanes, disease, famine, terrorism, homicide, suicide, immorality, incest, poverty, drugs…

The devil is no match for God! When the Spirit of God moves, things begin to happen. When God speaks, molecules and matter, blood cells and membranes, tissues and organs, land and sea, mortals and mammals all obey His command. We know this is true because God formed all of creation by the power of His Word, thus: "**And *God said*…**"

When God said, "Let there be light," Satan had to let it go and immediately there was light! When God said, "Let there be a firmament in the midst of the waters and let it divide the waters from the waters," Satan had to get back… and, without delay, there appeared the beautiful blue sky adorned with white, fluffy clouds.

When God said, "Let the waters under the heaven be gathered together unto one place and let the dry land appear," Satan's clutter ceased and instantly land, oceans, seas and rivers emerged. Child of God, when God speaks, all heaven and hell stand at attention awaiting His command!

When you know God, He'll speak life into your dead situation.

When you *really* know God, He'll bring order out of your chaos.

There is a Word for every circumstance; just stand on the power of God's Word! Simply remind God of His Word. Send the Word of God out into the atmosphere. When the enemy attacks you, just say, "God, you said…"

"Wait on the LORD, and keep his way, and he
shall
exalt thee to inherit the land: when the wicked
are cut off, thou shalt see it."
Psalms 37:34.

When in lack… "God, you said…"

"Delight thyself also in the LORD; and he shall
give thee the desires of thine heart."
Psalms 37:4

"But my God shall supply all your need
according
to his riches in glory by Christ Jesus."
Philippians 4:19.

When bills are overdue… God, you said…"

"I have been young, and now am old; yet have I
not
seen the righteous forsaken, nor his seed
begging bread."
Psalms 37:25;

"The young lions do lack, and suffer hunger:
but they that seek the LORD shall not want any
good thing."
Psalms 34:10.

When your children won't line up with the Word of
God… "God, you said…"

"His seed shall be mighty upon earth: the
generation
of the upright shall be blessed"
Psalms 112:2;

"The just man walketh in his integrity:
his children are blessed after him."

Proverbs 20:7.

When sickness attacks… "God, you said…"

"But he was wounded for our transgressions,
he
was bruised for our iniquities: the chastisement
of
our peace was upon him; and with his stripes
we are healed."
Isaiah 53:5.

When you've cried all night long… "God, you said
(through your servant)…"

"In my distress I called upon the LORD, and
cried unto my God: he heard my voice out of
his temple, and my cry came before him, even
into his ears."
Psalms 18:6

"The eyes of the LORD are upon the righteous,
and his ears are open unto their cry."
Psalms 34:15.

Child of God, I encourage you to desperately pursue
God. He's the lover of your soul, the prince of peace, light
in darkness, a doctor in the sickroom, a heavy load bearer,
comfort in time of sorrow, the great Eternal Wonder,
Zion's righteous Governor, the Holy Counselor, a lawyer
in the courtroom, peace in the midst of turmoil, the
commanding master of the universe, our Savior, our
deliverer and our soon coming King… His name is
JESUS!!!

If you don't know the Savior, if you haven't
developed a personal relationship with "the real star," I
urge you to pursue God. Face down and desperately seek
after Jesus, get acquainted with Him. We are living in
desperate times and if we are going to really know God,

we must pursue Him on purpose! You will never stumble upon a sincere, intimate relationship with God. You must do it on PURPOSE! It won't happen by accident!

The American Heritage dictionary defines desperate as, "having lost all hope; despairing, undertaken out of extreme urgency or as a last resort." Pursuit is defined as: "the act of chasing." God is looking for a few people who will urgently and desperately chase Him. A select few who aren't concerned about the way they look or what people think – they just want to know more of God. A people who desire greater anointing and greater power; a people who can lay hands on the sick and they are healed; a people who can rebuke demons and they flee; a people who can walk into a room and the anointing of God is so strong that His power is felt, without their even saying a word. This anointing is available for all who are willing to face down and pursue God!

Chapter Ten

Rise Up!!!!! This Is the Day!

> "Then Deborah said to Barak, "Up! For this is
> the day in which the LORD has delivered Sisera
> into your hand. Has not the LORD gone out
> before you?" So Barak went down from Mount
> Tabor with ten thousand men following him."
> Judges 4:14-16

Scripture tells us that, during this period of time, Israel was doing evil in the sight of God.

> "And the children of Israel again did evil in the
> sight of the LORD…"
> Judges 4:1

Israel had a habit of doing good for a while, but when they got around the wrong people, they would take on their ungodly ways. They still professed God, they still went to church on Sunday mornings, they still sang in the choir, they still ushered on the usher board, but on Monday through Saturday, they did everything that the world did.

I heard a story about a lady who was driving her car when another person cut in front of her and caused her to catch the stop light. The lady began to scream and cuss at the other driver. There just happened to be a policeman behind her. The police walked up to the car and actually handcuffed the lady and placed her in the back of his police car. After several minutes, the lady said, "Why in the world are you detaining me?…. Didn't you see that other car jump in front of me and almost cause an accident?"

By this time the police had run her ID and he apologized to her for the mistake. He went on to tell her that he just assumed that the car was stolen when he saw the "I love Jesus" bumper sticker, and the "Jesus saves" license plate! Clearly this lady was not acting as a Christian should act!

Now, I don't know if this is a true story or not, but I do know some cussing saints, some clubbing saints, some mean saints, some saints who look at pornography, some saints who are adulteresses, fornicators, whoremongers, homosexuals, lesbians, liars, haters. They still profess their love for Jesus, but they don't love Him enough to completely turn from wickedness. Child of God, may I submit to you that this is a dangerous place in which to be.

> "For the LORD your God is a consuming fire, a
> jealous God."
> Deuteronomy 4:24

> "So then, because you are lukewarm, and
> neither cold nor hot, I will vomit you out of My
> mouth."
> Revelation 3:16

Listen, don't do anything halfheartedly.... If you're going to play sports, be the best athlete you can be... If you're going to go to school, be the best student you can be... If you're going to be married, be the best husband or wife you can be... If you're going to have children, be the best parent you can be... I don't care what you do.... If you mop floors, be the best janitor you can be... If you work at McDonald's, be the best employee they have and if you're going to be a Christian, be the best Christian you can be!

Turn, turn from your evil ways! For why should you die, O house of Israel? For God we live and for God we die!

RISE UP!! THIS IS THE DAY!

We see in the Bible that God was angry with Israel because of their evil ways, therefore God delivered them into the hands of an evil king named Jabin. Scripture further states that for twenty years this evil king harshly oppressed the children of Israel. But after twenty long years of struggle, the Israelites finally cried out to God for mercy, and God heard them!

I don't understand why it always takes us so long to look to Jesus! There's even a song that says, "When you've tried everything and everything has failed, try Jesus!"

Why wait until everything has failed before you invite Jesus into the situation?

"…there is no other name under heaven given
among men by which we must be saved."
Acts 4:12

The name of Jesus will save you from eternal hell and His name will also save you from your present hell! Whatever the situation is, *God is able to do exceedingly, abundantly above all that we ask or think, according to the power that works in us…* and that POWER comes through HIS NAME JESUS!!!!

Some of us still haven't embraced the reality of the impact of our words…

"Death and life are in the power of the
tongue…"
Proverbs 18:21

We say things like, *I'm so tired… You make me sick… You get on my nerves… MY arthritis is cutting up…* Every time you look up there's something negative coming out of your mouth! Instead of looking at the positive in a situation, we always see the negative. Several years ago, my son was in and out of trouble… I couldn't keep him in school; he was staying out all hours of the night, hanging with the wrong crowds, going to school high off of marijuana ... It seemed like everything he did, he got caught.... The other people he was around who were doing the same things he was doing and even worse things, they never got caught; but the very time my son did anything wrong, he got caught. There's a message right there: When God has purpose and destiny for your life, when he has chosen you for His Kingdom... you can run, but you can't hide...

Look at Jonah: God had a job for him to do, and his disobedience landed him in the belly of a whale. Listen, your children are the heritage of God, and they can only go so far!!! My son kept getting into trouble, getting caught and getting in trouble, getting caught... until finally he landed in prison with a ten-year sentence on a drug charge. Now that's my baby boy, and that thing just ripped my heart out!!!! I was devastated for a minute until I got in the presence of God and He began to reveal some things to me.

The importance of getting in God's presence... not just going to church, not jumping and shouting... I'm talking about shutting up in a dark closet all by myself, lying prostrate on the floor (face down) for as long as it takes to hear God!

You may not have been there yet, but just keep living, there's coming a time in your life when you're going to have to shut off all the phones, turn the TV off and get into the presence of God! *For in the presence of God there is fullness of joy!*

And the joy of the Lord is your strength! When you operate in the joy of the Lord, you don't have time for negative thinking!

When one of my sons was a child, about 10 years old, he fell two stories hitting his head on a concrete floor. He went into a severe coma and the doctors thought he had developed spinal meningitis. The devil was trying to kill my son. But the saints began to pray!

We received the news on a Sunday morning and immediately my husband and I began to alert the saints to pray. My husband called his father who was pastoring a church in Little Rock, Arkansas, and my father-in-law stopped service and had the saints pray for my son. My husband called his uncle who pastored a church in Indianapolis; he stopped service and had the saints pray for my son. I called my mother and the saints in her church began to pray... The gates of heaven were being flooded with the prayers of the righteous on behalf of my son and Prayer Changes Things! Within twenty-four hours my son was totally healed! No coma, no trace of meningitis, no memory loss, no adverse symptoms... just plain HEALED!!!!

"For the eyes of the Lord are over the righteous,
and his ears are open unto their prayers..."
1Peter 3:12

Instead of focusing on worrying and stressing out, we must concentrate on God and on His people and on the work that He has assigned us to do.

"But you be watchful in all things, endure
afflictions, do the work of an evangelist, fulfill
your ministry."
2Timothy 4:5

That's what I love about Jesus! I don't care how far away you've strayed, I don't care what kind of mess you're in, I don't care what the doctors' report may be, I don't care what people have to say about you, all you have to do is call on JESUS! He will hear your cry! Late in the midnight hour just call on Jesus! Body racked with pain? Call on Jesus! Children acting crazy? Call on Jesus! Husband cutting up? Call on Jesus! Robbing Peter to pay Paul? Call on Jesus! **Come on Zion, take a praise break**

and shout Jesus!!!!   There IS power in HIS NAME!
JESUS!!!!

JESUS!!!!!

Some of you don't really understand what is
happening in the spirit realm when you call the name
Jesus! At the name of Jesus demons flee. At the name of
Jesus nations are transformed. The name of Jesus cures
cancer, At the name of Jesus angels stand at attention,
awaiting their assignment! The name of Jesus kept you in
your right mind! Jesus kept that bullet from taking you
out!!!

Jesus kept your mouth shut when you wanted to
cuss him out. **Shout JESUS!!!!!!**

Chapter Eleven

Don't Settle in Lodebar

Regardless of the circumstances that surround your life, you must not settle for anything less than what God has promised. I'm reminded of a little lame man, the grandson of King Saul and the son of Jonathan, named Mephibosheth. One piece of information transported Mephibosheth from underneath a table, where he was satisfied living in obscurity, rags and filth and eating crumbs, to the palace of King David. Many New Testament believers are a reflection of Mephibosheth. Many of them are unaware of the blessings and provisions of God in their lives and, most importantly, they don't know how to obtain those provisions.

Mephibosheth was only five years old when David became King. His nanny knew how Saul hated David and she was certain that David would have all of Saul's family killed. So this concerned nanny picked up Mephibosheth in her arms and went fleeing to Lodebar. While she was running with the child in her arms, she fell and broke both of his feet, thus causing him to be lame.

> "And Jonathan, Saul's son, had a son that was lame of his feet. He was five years old when the tidings came of Saul and Jonathan out of Jezreel, and his nurse took him up, and fled: and it came to pass, as she made haste to flee, that he fell, and became lame. And his name was Mephibosheth."
> 2Samuel 4:4

I feel the Spirit of God urging me to tell you, "Don't run, God has already made a way of escape!" Consider the following scripture:

> "Ye shall not need to fight in this battle:
> set yourselves, stand ye still, and see the
> salvation of the LORD with you..."
> 2Chronicles 20:17

You see, when you run from your problems, when you take things into your own hands, you will make a shambles of the situation every time. Just stand still! Stand on the promises of God! Mephibosheth's accident also alerts us to several other key points:

First, watch whom you associate with; second, watch whom you confide in; and third, be careful from whom you take counsel. Mephibosheth's nanny no doubt loved him, but she didn't know the will of God. Your unsaved friends may not mean you any harm, but they don't know the will of God and listening to their advice might spiritually lame you.

Lodebar... Allow me for a moment to take you on a journey to a place in the Old Testament known as Lodebar. Lodebar was a Samaritan slum, east of Jordan, in the land of Gilead. It was a place of lethargy, obscurity, depression, emptiness, barrenness, apathy and rejection. When we don't obey God's Word, when we refuse to fulfill our purpose, when we allow fear and intimidation to stop us from receiving God's covenant promises, we are forced to reside in the place of Lodebar. Child of God, many of us wear a smile and try to make people think we are living in Jerusalem, the city of prosperity; but we know, deep down inside, it's just Lodebar.

Several years passed and scripture lets us know that Mephibosheth ended up in the house of Machir, which means, "Sold Out." Many of us have sold out to our circumstances – we've allowed generational curses to lay claim in our families. We say, *Alcoholism runs in my family, cancer runs in my family, homosexuality runs in mu family, divorce, infidelity runs in my family, diabetes runs in my family…*

The devil is a liar and I come against generational curses in the name of Jesus; and by the authority of God I replace them with generational blessings. Your children will walk in righteousness… Your family will enjoy long life and health… Your seed will prosper.

Mephibosheth was hiding out because he knew David was coming for him at any moment. He lived under a constant cloud of fear, waiting for the king to come and kill him. One day one of King David's great captains entered his small shack and pulled the covers off of the table under which Mephibosheth hid and said, "The King hath need of you." Well, Mephibosheth fell at David's feet and said, 'I'm nothing but a dog".

> "And he bowed himself, and said, What is thy servant, that thou shouldest look upon such a dead dog as I am? "
> 2Samuel 9:8

In the Old Testament, wild dogs were unclean animals that wandered about devouring dead bodies and garbage off of the streets. To apply the term "dog" to oneself meant tremendous reproach and humiliation. You must understand that your opinion of who you are can draw you to the place called Lodebar. Stop judging yourself by your circumstances. Your mother's boyfriend may have sexually abused you, you may have dropped out of school in the sixth grade, you may have lived on the wrong side of the tracks. It really doesn't matter what obstacles you are facing; you can have what God says you can have; you can do what God says you can do; and you are who God says you are!

So… What does God say? God says that you are the head and not the tail;

> "And the LORD shall make thee the head, and
> not the tail; and thou shalt be above only"
> Deuteronomy 28:13

God says that you're more than a conqueror:

> "Nay, in all these things we are more than
> conquerors through him that loved us."
> Romans 8:37

God says you are a chosen generation; you are a royal priesthood:

> "But ye are a chosen generation, a royal
> priesthood, an holy nation"
> 1Peter 2:9

God says, you are an heir of God through Christ Jesus:

> "Wherefore thou art no more a servant, but a
> son;
> and if a son, then an heir of God through
> Christ."
> Galatians 4:7

God says you can ask and it shall be given:

> " Ask, and it shall be given you; seek, and ye
> shall find; knock, and it shall be opened unto
> you…"
> Matthew 7:7

God says you are a mountain mover:

> "…If ye have faith as a grain of mustard seed,
> ye shall say unto this mountain, Remove hence
> to yonder place; and it shall remove; and
> nothing shall be impossible unto you."
> Matthew 17:20

Enlarge your thinking! You are a child of the King! Increase your FAITH for without faith it is impossible to please the Lord!

"But without faith it is impossible to please
him: for he that cometh to God must believe
that he is, and that he is a rewarder of them that
diligently seek him."
Hebrews 11:6

As you read the following scriptures, please allow God's Word to thoroughly penetrate the deepest recesses of your heart and strengthen your faith:

"He staggered not at the promise of God
through unbelief; but was strong in faith, giving
glory to God;
21 And being fully persuaded that, what he
had promised, he was able also to perform."
Romans 4:20-21

"While we look not at the things which are
seen, but
at the things which are not seen: for the things
which are seen are temporal; but the things
which are not seen are eternal."
2Corinnthians 4:18

"And all things, whatsoever ye shall ask in
prayer, believing, ye shall receive."
Matthew 21:22

"But let him ask in faith, nothing wavering. For
he that wavereth is like a wave of the sea driven
with the wind and tossed. "
James 1:6

"For with God nothing shall be impossible."

Luke 1:37

Faith in God is developed through a consistent prayer life. There is a peace in God that can only be obtained through an intimate relationship with the Lord. Even in the natural, a fisherman may fish in the same spot all day and not catch a thing, but he continues to fish because he loves the peace and quiet and tranquility that comes with the sport. Even though he might not catch one fish all day, he still loves to fish because he knows eventually something is going to bite!

When you pray you may not receive what you are praying for right away, but there's a peace and contentment, there's a joy that comes when you get in God's presence. So, even though your prayers seem to go unanswered for a season, you continue to pray because through faith you know eventually something's going to happen... So you face down and PUSH; you Pray Until Something Happens!

A fisherman knows exactly what kind of bait to use when he is trying to get a certain kind of fish. If he's fishing for BASS he might use LURES.

If he's trying to catch catfish, he'll use night crawlers, liver or shrimp. He's not casting out a lure to catch a bluegill.

I've seen two people fishing in the same lake, side by side, and one is catching big fat, juicy fish and the other is catching nothing!

You must understand that just because the fisherman can't see the fish and just because he is not catching anything doesn't mean that there's nothing in the lake. I've seen lakes where there are large schools of fish just swimming along the sides of the bank. When this occurs all you need is a net to swoop them up! That's what you call an easy catch; but there are times, usually in the heat of the day that the fish go deep in order to stay cool and the fisherman must put a heaver anchor on his line so his bait can go deep in order to catch the fish. If he left the lightweight anchor on the bait, it would simply float on the top of the water.

There will be times when you pray and immediately your prayers are answered. But there will be times when your prayers seem to be going unheard – there will be times that your prayers seem to bounce off the walls, there will be times that you wonder if God is listening to you at all. But you must understand that there are things that God has for you that you will never receive until you anchor yourself, face down and go deep!

When you want results for specific issues, pray the Word of God! Remind God of His Word and bind Him to it! There are times when the fisherman has the right bait, he's gone deep, but the fish is too big for his line. So when the fish bites, the line breaks and the catch gets away. Some prayers are being ignored in the spirit realm and are not answered right now because God knows you aren't strong enough to hold on to it, He knows you can't handle it…

Don't stop praying: just realize that God has to strengthen you and mold and shape you and work some things out of you before He can bless you. No good thing will HE withhold from them that walk uprightly before Him. Don't stop praying for a husband – just realize that before God can bless you with one, you've got to learn how to be submissive or you'll end up in divorce and that's not a good thing! Don't stop praying for spiritual discernment; just realize that before God can bless you with this gift, He's got to break you from gossiping or you'll tell everybody's business… Don't stop praying for the gift of laying on of hands and healing, but realize that before He can grant you this gift, he's got to break you of your pride or you'll try to take God's glory…

Don't stop praying for prosperity; just realize that your stingy spirit has to be dealt with first... Don't stop praying... Don't stop pushing... but while you're waiting on your blessing, ask the Lord to cleanse you, so that when He blesses you, you

won't blow it!

Think of a leer jet... When you fly on a jet you're moving so fast that you can't even feel it. It feels like you are standing still when you are literally flying. Sometimes getting off the ground is the hardest thing to do. Snow makes the runway slick; storms limit visibility and prevent the planes from taking off... But, if you can just take off the ground, you can soar above all of it – you can fly so high that you don't even realize what the weather is like below.

When you learn to soar above the mess, it won't faze you. All hell can be breaking out in the natural realm, but you must learn to operate in the spirit realm and rise above what your situation looks like... "Not by power nor by might, but by my spirit," saith the Lord.

Whether you travel in an auto or a leer jet, the distance remains the same, but in a jet you get to your destination much quicker. You are more comfortable; you get to eat and drink and see movies, go to the restroom. It costs you a little more, but it is worth all of the added benefits.

It may cost you some friends to soar with Jesus, but it's worth it! It may cost you some meals... it may cost you some fun and entertainment... it may cost you time... it may cost you the latest gossip... it may cost you your favorite TV show, but you will simply have to get face down in prayer and consecrate yourself to God in order to operate in overflow!

Chapter Twelve

"Too Strong for Too Long"

"And Naomi said to her two daughters-in-law,
'Go, return each to her mother's house. The
LORD deal kindly with you, as you have dealt
with the dead and with me.
9 "The LORD grant that you may find rest, each
in
the house of her husband.' Then she kissed
them,
and they lifted up their voices and wept."
Ruth 1:8-9

"But Ruth said: 'Entreat me not to leave you, Or
to turn back from following after you; For
wherever you go, I will go; And wherever you
lodge, I will lodge; Your people shall be my
people, And your God, my God.
17 Where you die, I will die, And there will I be
buried.
The LORD do so to me, and more also,
If anything but death parts you and me.'"
Ruth 1:16-17

"We Been Too Strong for Too Long and I Can't Live Without You" Some of you recognize this as lyrics from a song by Mary J. Blige. She goes on to say in the song, "I'll be waiting up until you get home, because I can't sleep without you, baby." Well, Miss Mary is talking about her love for a man; she is expressing her strong level of dependence on her lover.

But in this chapter I will reflect upon the love and the total need that the child of God has for the Lord Jesus Christ, "For in Him we live, and move, and have our being..." Come hell or high water... We Been Too Strong For Too Long! In sickness and pain.... We Been Too Strong For Too Long. Friends may walk out on me but... We Been Too Strong For Too Long!

I may have to cry all night long but, We Been Too Strong For Too Long and can't no devil in hell make me turn my back on my Savior. You see, my joy is not predicated on what my circumstances look like... This joy I have – the world didn't give it and the world can't take it away!

As we examine our text at this point, we read about Elimelech and his wife Naomi leaving Bethlehem because of a famine in the land. They leave Bethlehem with their two sons and move to the country of Moab, a place of plenty, but a place where heathens lived and where the people worshiped false Gods.

It is important that we realize that God had given the Jewish people their promised land, Israel, and He promised to provide for their needs. But when things got a little rough, Elimelech cut out in spite of God's promise. Instead of standing on God's Word, instead of trusting God to supply their needs, they chose to set up camp with the Moabites.

Child of God, I don't care how bad things may seem, I'd rather be poor and have Jesus, than be rich without Him...

> "For what profit is it to a man if he gains the
> whole world, and loses his own soul? Or what
> will a man
> give in exchange for his soul?"
> Matthew 16:26

I'd rather struggle and have Jesus than ease through without Him... I'd rather walk with Jesus than ride without Him... I don't care how rough things get... don't get weary in the place that God has set you!

"And let us not grow weary while doing good,
for in due season we shall reap if we do not lose
heart."
Galatians 6:9

"But ye, brethren, be not weary in well doing."
2Thimothy 3:13

The book of Psalms picks it up and says,

"Wait on the Lord, be of Good courage and He
shall
strengthen thine heart, Wait I say on the Lord!"
Psalms 27:14

You Been Too Strong For Too Long... and You Can't Live Without HIM!   for *He is* the Way, *He is* the Truth and *He is* the Life!!!!!!

"Jesus saith unto him, I am the way, the truth,
and the life: no man cometh unto the Father,
but by me."
John 14:6

I don't care what you have to let go of, HOLD ONTO GOD; your very life depends on it!!!

Our text says that shortly after Elimelech and his family moved to Moab, Elimelech died, leaving Naomi his wife a widow with two sons. Scripture goes on to say that Naomi's two sons married Moabite women, Ruth and Orpah and, after about ten years, both sons died leaving no children. So we see this family, when faced with opposition, leaving God's place of promise; we see them leaving the place where God had positioned them; we see them looking at the sinners, looking at the world and thinking they would be better off on the other side. We see them going against the law of God and bringing Moabite women into their family and, as a result of their actions, within ten years every man in their family is dead! The family seed is destroyed!

It is important that we realize the significance of all of the men dying in their family. Even in our society today, the devil has attacked the men, attempting to kill off all of our men because he knows that if he can kill our men, he can cripple our families and abort purpose and destiny.

Hear this: I know that some of you may have been abused, mistreated, raped, violated, cheated on and torn down by a man, but regardless of how you may have been treated, God still ordained men to be the head. And the devil knows that if men ever rise up and take their rightful place in the Kingdom of God, all hell will break loose! Every time I look at the news and see our men killing each other, our men locked up in prison, our men who have no respect for themselves or for God, our men who don't have a clue of who they really are and what they are purposed to become – my heart grieves for our MEN!

When I look at some of our mega ministries and see how the devil has attacked great men and women of God, attempting to destroy the integrity of the church, my heart grieves for this world! Women, I don't care how independent you may be, you must realize the importance of a man... Women, we have got to cover our men in prayer!

So now, Naomi had lost everything... her husband and her two sons and her property because in those days women couldn't own property. She finally decides to return to Bethlehem.

Why is it that sometimes God has to strip us of everything to get our attention? When things are going good, we just can't find time to face down and pray, but let trouble come knocking on our door and we go down on our face for hours. When we're feeling good, we come to church on Sundays most of the time, but when the doctor gives a bad report, we're at church every time the doors open. We're judgmental and critical of everybody and everything when our families are doing well, but the minute trouble hits our home, we become more compassionate and sympathetic towards others. Isn't it odd how trouble has a way of turning us toward God? Isn't it odd how trouble has a way of humbling you?

As Naomi is leaving Moab, her two son's wives, Orpah and Ruth, leave with her, but Naomi tells them to go back to Moab, to their mother's homes so that they could eventually remarry, have children and live happy fulfilled lives.

Scripture says that while the girls cried and appeared to really love Naomi, Orpah finally agreed to go back to Moab. You see, Orpah couldn't see the big picture. She couldn't see beyond her immediate circumstance. All she could see was three, confused, grieving, poor widows. Orpah was not fully committed; she loved Naomi, but not enough to forsake all in order to be with her.

The same is true with some Christians today. They love Jesus, but they will only go so far to be with Him. When the stakes get too high, they cut out! They want all of the glorious things that God has prepared for His children, but they aren't willing to go through anything to get it. At the first sight of trouble they cut out! Trouble in the church… they leave and go to another church or don't go at all. Trouble in the marriage… they divorce. Trouble on the job… they quit!

God is telling me to tell somebody to stop dwelling in the hurt of your past and possess the promise of your future! Yeah… the devil came to steal and to kill, but guess what… YOU'RE STILL HERE!!!! In case you didn't know, the devil can't kill you because it's a fixed fight and the Word of God has given us insight into the future and we have already won! Now's the time to stop living in lack and move into your Abundance!

Ruth refused to leave Naomi. Scripture says Ruth cleaved to Naomi.

Ruth said: 'Don't ask me to go back... for wherever you go, I'm going; wherever you lodge, I'm lodging... Your people shall be my people, and your God, my God."

In other words, "Where you die, I'm gonna die, and nothing but death is going to separate me and you 'cause We Been Too Strong For Too Long and I Can't Live Without You!

Ruth was determined to hang in there for the long haul! Ruth saw in Naomi what Naomi couldn't even see in herself. Listen, child of God, even in your worst hour the world sees that you are blessed. It may seem that God has forsaken you... It may seem that your prayers are falling on deaf ears... It may seem that you're going nowhere fast... but one thing you can take to the bank and that is that God will never leave you nor forsake you!

I don't care how far you've strayed, I don't care what you have done, I don't care what situation you may find yourself in, I don't care who says you'll never make it... we serve a God who is able to do exceedingly and abundantly above all that we can ever ask or think and He specializes in the impossible! And even though you may be down, you're not out! God still has a purpose and a plan for your life!

> "For the Lord GOD will help me; Therefore I
> will not be disgraced; Therefore I have set my
> face like a flint, And I know that I will not be
> ashamed."
> Isaiah 50:7

Get up out of Moab, go back to the place of promise... You been too strong for too long and God is not though with you yet!

So when Naomi and Ruth got back to Bethlehem, the people there were glad to see Naomi and they began to call her name which means "sweetness," but she told them to call her name Mara, which means "bitterness" because the Lord had dealt bitterly with her.

You see, back then a person's name meant something. The name Ruth meant a female friend, and she held true to her name. Today we name our children any old thing... Nae-Nae, Bay-Bay... and they sound real cute, but what does it mean? Every time you say your child's name out loud you are speaking something out over their lives... What are you declaring over your children?

Speak life over your children, not curses... It may be too late to rename your child, but it's not too late to begin to speak blessings over them. When you call your daughter say, "Nae-Nae... virtuous woman of God... get off of the telephone and finish your homework!" "Nae-Nae, divinely favored, go do the dishes!"

When you address your son say, "Bay-Bay, great man of valor, go take out the trash!" "Bay-Bay, mighty prayer warrior... be home before curfew!" Speak life over your family; set the course for their future.

It's important that we realize that Ruth didn't hang onto her mother-in-law to be a burden to her; she wanted to be a blessing. As soon as Ruth got to Judah she went straight to work by gleaning the fields. When they arrived it was the beginning of the barley season and when the fields were harvested the farmers would leave the remnants for the widows and the poor to pick up.

Boaz, who was a very wealthy and reputable man, notices Ruth while she is working in his field. Note that Ruth didn't go to Bethlehem and start murmuring and complaining about what they didn't have. She didn't go put on a low cut dress with a split clear up her side to try to entice a man. She didn't go to the market and steal food. She didn't go get some weed to sell. She didn't stand in the streets and beg. NO, Ruth was focused on being a blessing to her mother-in-law, and she went to work and the Bible says that, while she was focused on her task, Boaz inquired of her, he noticed her.

There's a message right there. Women of God, you don't have to go out of your way to be noticed; just stay focused and keep working in the Kingdom and your Boaz will inquire of you! When Boaz approached Ruth, she asked him, "Why did you take notice of me?"

He told her, "I've heard all about you and the way that you are taking care of your mother-in-law. I've heard how you have taken on our God and our customs... not to mention that you look good too... yea, I heard about you..."

Now this is for all of the young people out there: I can imagine Boaz looking at Ruth and saying, "Shawty is a TEN!"

Listen, young people, your reputation will precede you. This is for the young ladies: the decisions that you make now will follow you the rest of your life! I don't care how much he says he loves you, make him wait.

Scripture goes on to tell us that Boaz marries Ruth and not only redeems her position in society, but establishes her position in the lineage of our Lord and Savior Jesus Christ! Listen, you will never do more for others than God will give back to you! I heard one of the young people say that the going thing now in the club is to "Make It Rain"! I asked what in the world is making it rain? They told me that making it rain is when people go into the club and throw big wads of money in the air and let it fall to the ground like rain. And who ever gets the money keeps the money.

Well, that blew my mind... I say we need to come into the house of God and make it rain! What has the club done for you to deserve that kind of rain? God woke you up this morning; God started you on your way; God put food on your table; God kept you in your right mind; God kept that bullet from hitting you while you were in the club making it rain... If you gonna make it rain... make it rain in the house of the Lord!! Don't ever forget where your blessings come from!

Stop following after the devil's mess! Face down in prayer; stick close to God, 'cause You Been Too Strong For Too Long and You Can't Live Without HIM!

Chapter Thirteen

Prayer, a Magnet to Revelation

When you begin to face down in prayer, God will usher you to new levels of wisdom and understanding and He will give you great insight and revelation. God will show you things that can only be seen through spending intimate time with the Savior. Prayer is like a magnet to revelation... the more that you pray, the more you understand the mind of Christ. The following are revelations the Lord showed me while face down:

DREAM 1

I saw a vision of a young lady, light skinned with long hair.... She was sitting on a stool, crying and pleading with her husband. Her husband was trying to get her to defecate and urinate and pass gas in front of him, but she refused to do it. The husband told her, "I do it around you so you should do it around me." But the wife wouldn't do it because she was extremely uncomfortable.

Then I saw another vision of three people in a bath tub together. One was a husband, the other was his wife and the other was their son (about 9 years old). The boy is the same male that was in the previous vision, except in the other vision he was an adult. This family was covered in human feces and naked in the tub. The wife was lying on top of her husband and they were French kissing. As they kissed, feces were going into their mouths, but it didn't bother them at all; they kept right on kissing as though the mess was not even on them.

While the mother and father were kissing, the little boy was frantically trying to reach underneath his mother so he could get to her breast. But there was so much manure that, every time he attempted to grab her, his hands kept slipping off of her.

Then I awoke. I was very confused because I had no idea what this dream meant, however I knew that it was not just a dream to be dismissed as nothing, I knew that there was relevance to this dream so I went face down and asked God for clarification. God led me to scriptures in the Bible that I had never read before. The following are the scriptures that God took me to:

> 5 "For I have laid upon thee the years of their iniquity, according to the number of the days, three hundred and ninety days: so shalt thou bear
> the iniquity of the house of Israel.
> 12 And thou shalt eat it as barley cakes, and thou shalt bake it with dung that cometh out of man, in their sight.
> 13 And the LORD said, Even thus shall the children of Israel eat their defiled bread among the Gentiles, whither I will drive them.
> 14 Then said I, Ah Lord GOD! behold, my soul hath not been polluted: for from my youth up even till now have I not eaten of that which dieth of itself, or is torn in pieces; neither came there abominable flesh into my mouth.
> 15 Then he said unto me, Lo, I have given thee cow's dung for man's dung, and thou shalt prepare thy bread therewith.
> 17 That they may want bread and water, and be astonied one with another, and consume away for their iniquity."
> Ezekiel 4:5, 12-15, 17

After reading the scripture the Lord showed me that he hates sin and the only way that he could allow us to see how much he abhors sin is to associate it with feces (*waste matter eliminated from bowels*). Feces emit strong foul odors and are highly offensive. Feces are nasty and carry diseases. In Ezekiel 4 we see that the Israelites were grossly immoral and wicked and God laid their sins on Ezekiel. God commanded Ezekiel to bake with human feces which represented His level of disgust for sin.

Ezekiel was so despondent at the Lord's command that God eventually allowed Ezekiel to use cow manure instead. God showed me that He hates sin, the same way that we would hate feces being shoved into our mouths!

The Lord gave me further revelation regarding my vision:

This is what God said to me: In the first vision the feces represented sin. The husband's request represented a generation of sin and perversion. Because he was raised in sin, he was sucked into it and he didn't even realize that what he was doing was wrong. He had no concept of right versus wrong and he was comfortable with sin.

The woman, on the other hand, represented righteousness. She was able to discern right from wrong and she was very uncomfortable around sin. The interaction between the two of them represented the constant war between good and evil and how the enemy will tempt the saints to do wrong. That's why we should always pray:

> "And lead us not into temptation, but deliver
> us from evil: For thine is the kingdom, and the
> power, and the glory, for ever."
> Matthew 6:13

In the second vision, the feces also represent sin. The fact that feces were all over the couple, even in their mouths, and they still didn't notice it, represented seared consciousness towards sin (a high tolerance for sin). The 9-year old boy reaching for his mother's breast represented the fact that children of all ages still crave for nourishment from their mother. Mothers are the nurturers and they have the innate ability to rear a child and literally set the course for his/her life.

DREAM 2

In a dream I saw people shooting at me with long guns. These people were mounted high on horses. Their gun shots were coming at me from every angle. At first I was darting the bullets successfully, but eventually a bullet hit me straight in my heart. In my mind I was certain that the bullet was going to kill me, but to my surprise, I was not injured at all. The bullet didn't even faze me! In fact, after I was hit, I was able to get to the actual enemy that had shot me.

I raised my hand and directed it towards him and began pleading the blood of Jesus! When I said, "In Jesus Name," at that very moment the enemy began to bend down as if he were being weakened. Now I had him in a vulnerable state, a position where I could kill him. Just as I was about to destroy the enemy, God said, "NO! You are not supposed to kill; you're job is to restore!"

I didn't realize at the time that God was speaking to me prophetically. Following this dream, several months later, the very individual that tried to destroy my marriage called me on the phone and I had to counseel her and encourage her. Satan has presented me with countless opportunities to tear down and destroy the very individuals that have hurt me the most, but God has commanded me to restore His people! Consider the following scriptures:

"But I say unto you, That ye resist not evil: but
whosoever shall smite thee on thy right cheek,
turn to him the other also. "
Matthew5:39

"But I say unto you, Love your enemies, bless
them that curse you, do good to them that hate
you, and pray for them which despitefully use
you, and persecute you;"
Matthew 5:44

"But I say unto you which hear, Love your
enemies,
do good to them which hate you"
Luke 6:27

"Brethren, if a man be overtaken in a fault, ye
which
are spiritual, restore such an one in the spirit of
meekness; considering thyself, lest thou also be
tempted. "
Galatians 6:1

DREAM 3

I saw a young man who was about 17 years old. This
teenager was extremely distraught. He was holding a
loaded gun to his head and he was threatening to blow his
brains out! I pleaded with the young man and I begged
him not to kill himself. God actually gave me the man's
name, it was Derrick. Even though I actually called
Derrick by his name, he kept crying frantically and saying
he was going to shoot! That was the end of that scene.

Immediately, the next scene I saw was the San
Francisco- Oakland Bay Bridge. This bridge is called the
Golden Gate Bridge, but in my vision I saw it as a symbol

of sexual immorality, just like Sodom and Gomorrah. Then God spoke in my spirit that I must face down and pray and come against the spirit of homosexuality in our churches, in our families, in our communities and intercede for the city of San Francisco. I was instructed to come against the spirit of homosexuality and lesbianism that has infiltrated San Francisco. Just as He was displeased with the evil spirit that infiltrated Sodom, He is displeased with the wicked spirit that has set up camp in San Francisco.

"And there came two angels to Sodom at even; and Lot sat in the gate of Sodom: and Lot seeing them rose up to meet them; and he bowed himself with his face toward the ground;
2 And he said, Behold now, my lords, turn in, I pray you, into your servant's house, and tarry all night, and wash your feet, and ye shall rise up early, and go on your ways. And they said, Nay; but we will abide in the street all night.
3 And he pressed upon them greatly; and they turned in unto him, and entered into his house; and he made them a feast, and did bake unleavened bread, and they did eat.
4 But before they lay down, the men of the city, even the men of Sodom, compassed the house round, both old and young, all the people from every quarter:
5 And they called unto Lot, and said unto him, Where are the men which came in to thee this night?
bring them out unto us, that we may know them.
6 And Lot went out at the door unto them, and shut the door after him,
7 And said, I pray you, brethren, do not so wickedly."

Genesis 19:1-7

24 "Then the LORD rained upon Sodom and
upon Gomorrah brimstone and fire from the
LORD out of heaven;"
Genesis 19:24

28 "And he [Abraham] looked toward Sodom
and Gomorrah, and toward all the land of the
plain, and beheld, and, lo, the smoke of the
country went up as the smoke of a furnace."
Genesis 19:28

God is not pleased with the way our world is turning
further and further away from Him and His ways. Our
government officials have removed prayer from schools,
legalized gay marriages, gay priests are now being
ordained, gay couples are raising families as if that's the
way God intended it to be, homicides are escalating, child
abuse is on the rise… all types of evil prevail. We must
remember that God destroyed an entire city because He
couldn't find ten righteous people in it.

"And he said, Oh let not the Lord be angry, and
I will speak yet but this once: Peradventure ten
shall be found there. And he said, I will not
destroy it for ten's sake."
Genesis 18:32

I believe that the only thing that is holding the wrath
of God from destroying the United States of America is the
prayers of the righteous. I believe that God has a body of
true believers here on earth who are carrying out His will
and we are literally delaying the judgment of God. We all
have family members, friends, and love ones who need to
be set free from the chains of darkness. Please continue to
face down in prayer, cry out to God on the behalf of your
family so that they will be saved before God's judgment

strikes! It's only a matter of time... His coming is soon. Don't let it be said too late!

Chapter Fourteen

The Midnight Hour

The phrase "the midnight hour" is sometimes used to depict a struggle or a trying period in one's life. Midnight literally denotes the ending of one day and the beginning of another. Scripture reveals that Paul and Silas were experiencing both translations of the midnight hour. They were experiencing great ridicule and torture and they were worshiping late at night. But through their dedication and faith in God, they birthed a miracle in their midnight hour!

Scripture says that the Apostles were taken to a public place and accused of destroying public peace and endangering public safety. In essence, they were lied on. The multitude rose up against them and the magistrates tore off their clothes and beat them with rods and whips. After they had been severely beaten, they were thrown into the inner part of the prison... the darkest and most secure cell... the dungeon, if you will. As if this were not enough, their feet were placed in stocks that drastically stretched their legs! And they were chained like animals.

> 22"And the multitude rose up together against them: and the magistrates rent off their clothes, and commanded to beat them.
> 23 And when they had laid many stripes upon them,
> they cast them into prison, charging the jailor to keep them safely:
> 24 Who, having received such a charge, thrust them into the inner prison, and made their feet fast in the stocks."
> Acts 16:22-24

Just imagine the agony they must have suffered! But in spite of how they felt, in spite of what their situation looked like, in spite of the enemy's plans... the Bible says that at midnight Paul and Silas sang praises to God.

> 25 "And at midnight Paul and Silas prayed, and
> sang praises unto God: and the prisoners heard
> them.
> 26 And suddenly there was a great earthquake,
> so that the foundations of the prison were
> shaken: and immediately all the doors were
> opened, and every one's bands were loosed."
> Acts 16:25-26

Although midnight is a time when most people are fast asleep, we see that it is at midnight that Paul and Silas faced down and prayed and sang praises to God! Even though their bodies were racked with pain, even though they had great reason to fear, they remained focused on their true source of strength. Paul said,

> "I take pleasure in infirmities, in reproaches, in
> necessities, in persecutions, in distresses for
> Christ's sake: for when I am weak, then am I
> strong."
> 2Corinthians 12:10

The Bible said that right in the midst of their trouble, Paul and Silas prayed and sang praises to God! The Bible goes on to say that they not only sang, but they sang so loudly that the prisoners throughout the entire prison could hear them.

They turned a porch of death and a gate of hell into a sanctuary of praise! With bleeding backs and in a comfortless posture they sang like angels, and made the grim prison walls ring! No groans and moans were heard, but a nocturnal, jubilant sound such as that dungeon never echoed with before.

Paul and Silas were not intimidated by the devils mess! They didn't care what people thought! They were not ashamed of the Gospel of Jesus Christ!

The Bible tells us that when they faced down and prayed and praised... God began to move! If we are going to be powerful children of God, we must develop a sincere love of prayer. Prayer is an act of worship... Prayer is an act of devotion... Prayer is an act of confession... Prayer is an act of praise... Prayer is an act of thanksgiving... Prayer is a reverent petition made to God... Prayer is an act of communion with God where you talk to Him and He talks back to you... Prayer is your lifeline, your heavenly connection to your Father!

How can you love someone you really don't know? How can you really know someone with whom you never spend time? How can there be relationship with no intimacy? When you really know God, you will have supernatural power! When you really know God, you will can walk into a room and not say a word and your very presence will change the atmosphere! When you really know God, you don't have to get upset and all bent out of shape when the enemy throws things your way... you can just speak to that demonic rascal and he must flee! When you really know God, other people's lives will be effected by your anointing!

Saints, if you really want to see the power of God in action, begin to pray and praise! If you want deliverance, Pray and Praise... If you want to see the lives of those around you change... Pray and Praise! The Bible said that when they Praised, God caused the earth to quake as it had never done before. When they Praised... chains fell off! When they Praised... stocks were loosed! When they Praised... prison doors were opened! When they Praised... sinners listened! When they Praised... all of the prisoners around them were loosed! When they Praised... souls were saved!

There's Power in your Praise! Praise while you are yet suffering, Praise while you are still going through. Praise while everything seems hopeless. Praise while you feel bound. Praise while it seems that the enemy has the upper hand. Praise while everything seems to be going wrong...

Your praise excites the angelic host... Your praise puts a smile on God's face... Your praise shakes the very foundation of hell... Your praise terrifies the devil...

Your praise proclaims deliverance to the captives... Your praise opens prison doors to them that are bound... Your praise sets at liberty them that are bruised...

If you want to see the power of God in action... begin to PRAISE! PRAISE!!!!! PRAISE!!!!! PRAISE!!!!! Come on and "Give God PRAISE!"

Saints, use what you've got to get what you want!

The Bible says that when the jailor saw that all of the prisoners' chains had been loosed and that their cells had been opened, he fell down before the Apostles and cried, "What must I do to be saved!"

The jailor was so convinced that Paul and Silas were true men of God that he took them to his house, washed their wounds, gave them food and was ultimately saved along with his entire family. Understand that the same man who bound them in chains and stocks ultimately fell at their feet for mercy. The same man who severely beat them ended up taking them into his home... The same man who harshly persecuted them ended up washing their wounds. The same man who threw them into the inner prison, ended up feeding them from his own table.

"The LORD said unto my Lord, Sit thou at my right hand, until I make thine enemies thy footstool."
Psalms 110:1

David declared in the Psalm above that if we stay with the Lord, God will make our enemies our footstool. Don't try to get back at the enemy... Praise is your weapon... Don't plot your revenge... Praise is your weapon... Don't retaliate against the person who did you wrong... Praise is your weapon... Don't harbor hatred and bitterness... Praise is your weapon!

Chapter Fifteen

Prayer = Good Health

I would be remiss if I didn't stress the importance of prayer in sustaining good health. We must realize that healthy foods, vitamins and minerals, exercise, adequate rest and sufficient water consumption are very important to sustaining good health, but when they are combined with prayer, the impact is greatly enhanced. There are numerous scriptures supporting the use of prayer for healing. Even when death was prophesied by Isaiah, through prayer Hezekiah was granted an extension on life. The full account may be found in 2 Kings 20.1-7. It is synopsized below:

> "In those days was Hezekiah sick unto death.
> And the prophet Isaiah came to him, and said,
> Thus saith the LORD, thou shalt die, and not
> live.
> Then he turned his face to the wall, and <u>prayed
> unto the LORD…</u> And it came to pass, afore
> Isaiah was gone out into the middle court, that
> the word of the LORD came to him, saying,
> Turn again, and tell Hezekiah thus saith the
> LORD, <u>I have heard thy prayer, I have seen thy
> tears: behold, I will heal thee…</u> And I will add
> unto thy days fifteen years; and I will deliver
> thee…"

Hezekiah's disease was of a malignant nature and would have killed him if not for the healing power of prayer. Because of Hezekiah's prayer, God stopped the hand of death and added fifteen years to his life. God heard Hezekiah's prayer, He saw his tears and He healed him.

Notice that Hezekiah turned his face to the wall. Some say Hezekiah turned and faced the temple. Others say that he simply went into deep concentration, but I believe that Hezekiah turned away from all of the people that were in the room. He turned away from all of the doubters and nay-sayers; he didn't want to look at anything or anyone that could possibly distract him and ultimately prevent him from getting through to his God. He didn't want to hear anybody saying,

"Why you prayin' now? God done already said that you are going to die! Isaiah done already told you what God said… it's too late to pray now."

Child of God, we learn from Hezekiah that it is never too late to seek God's face. And when you are desperately seeking Gods face, you don't have time to have anybody else's face in the way. When you are face down, all you see is God!

Also notice that Hezekiah told God what he would do for God if he were delivered. What are you seeking God for, what are you believing God for? But what are you going to give back to God? What's in it for God? How is God going to get the glory out of your healing? How is God going to get the glory out of your financial breakthrough?

Although God miraculously delivered Hezekiah, Isaiah acted as his physician, if you will, by prescribing an outward medical application. Isaiah instructed that a lump of figs be laid on Hezekiah's boil.

> "And Isaiah said, Take a lump of figs. And they
> took and laid it on the boil, and he recovered."
> 2Ki 20:7

This medical application ripened the boil and brought it to a head so that the disease could be discharged. Now, we must understand that the medical application would have done no good had God not healed Hezekiah first. Because God said that Hezekiah would die and not live. We must also take note that the medical application was indeed administered. We cannot ignore this fact. Even in Biblical days medicine had its place in the healing process. It is our responsibility to get regular checkups and to adhere to our physician's advice.

Doctors and medicines are not to be despised, but rather viewed as one of God's many gifts to mankind. While we respect the medical field, we must not depend on it. Our hope must be in Jesus, "For in him we live, and move, and have our being…" (Acts 17:28)

For centuries, people have used prayer for their health concerns. Supporting research in this area is the National Center for Complementary and Alternative Medicine (NCCAM). Catherine Stoney Ph.D., a Program Officer in NCCAM's Division of Extramural Research and Training, says, "Scientists are investigating the connection between prayer and health outcomes and studies show some evidence that prayer is associated with health and mortality." (Stoney n.d.)

She went on to say that studies show that prayer can enhance immune function, cardiovascular function and other physiological changes and that praying for somebody who is ill, can actually make them better. (Kemper KJ n.d.) People all over the world are praying and getting results. Prayer is so powerful that even scientists are taking notice. Although prayer research is in its infancy, scientists and scholars from some of the world's most prestigious medical schools and universities are intrigued by the overwhelming correlation between prayer and healing.

Dr. Anne McCaffrey of the Harvard Medical School conducted a survey of 2,000 Americans and found that faith is a critical part of health care for many and that one-third of Americans are using PRAYER FOR HEALING. (McCaffrey AM n.d.) The survey results found that of the one-third using prayer to address health concerns, 75 percent pray for general wellness, 22 percent pray for help with a specific medical condition like cancer and 69 percent said prayer was helpful. ("Prayer for Health Concerns") Even the most skeptical scientists are admitting that prayer may be another powerful tool that can't be ignored.

A study carried out by the University of Maryland in the US has found prayer and spiritual healing may reduce pain and speed up the recovery of patients. More than half of these studies (57%) found a positive impact on patients. Dr Austin, an assistant professor on the university's complementary medicine program said, "In one study of nearly 1,000 heart patients, those who were being prayed for without their knowledge suffered 10% fewer complications." ("Prayer For Health Concerns")

Dr. Elizabeth Bowman, psychiatrist and clinical professor in the Department of Neurology in Indiana University's School of Medicine on the Indianapolis campus, cited one particular study which showed that people who attended worship services regularly were at lower risk of developing cardiovascular and artery diseases than those who rarely or do not attend services. She also stated that studies suggest that people who are grounded spiritually have an advantage in maintaining their health and halting the progression of serious illness. (Bowen n.d.)

Don't stop praying... Don't underestimate the power of Prayer... God is still a prayer answering God!

> "The eyes of the LORD are upon the righteous,
> and his ears are open unto their cry.
> The righteous cry, and the LORD heareth,
> and delivereth them..."

Psalms 34:15,17

Although this research is interesting, I really don't need scientific data to prove that prayer works... I'm a living testimony! Whatever your ailment may be, don't stop praying... don't underestimate the power of prayer...

Chapter Sixteen

P U S H
Pray Until Something Happens

1 "And he spake a parable unto them to this end,
that men ought always to pray, and not to faint;
2 Saying, There was in a city a judge, which
feared not God, neither regarded man:
3 And there was a widow in that city;
and she came unto him, saying,
Avenge me of mine adversary.
4 And he would not for a while: but
afterward he said within himself,
Though I fear not God, nor regard man;
5 Yet because this widow troubleth me,
I will avenge her, lest by her
continual coming she weary me.
6 And the Lord said, Hear
what the unjust judge saith.
7 And shall not God avenge his own elect,
which cry day and night unto him,
though he bear long with them?
8 I tell you that he will avenge them speedily.
Nevertheless when the Son of man cometh,
shall he find faith on the earth?"
Luke 18:1-8

Each year, the women at our church host a "Daddy's Girls PUSH Conference" because we realize the importance of persevering in prayer. As I consider people in the Bible who PUSHED, several individuals come to mind:

1.   The WOMAN WITH THE ISSUE OF BLOOD suffered for 12 long years but when she pushed through the crowd to get to Jesus, immediately she was healed!

> 43 "And a woman having an issue of blood
> twelve years, which had spent all her living
> upon physicians, neither could be healed of
> any,
> 44 Came behind him, and touched the border
> of his garment: and immediately her
> issue of blood stanched."
> Luke 8:43-44

2.   HANNAH was BARREN for many years, but through her PUSH, the curse was broken and she received her son Samuel…

> 9 "So Hannah rose up after they had eaten in
> Shiloh,
> and after they had drunk. Now Eli the priest
> sat upon a seat by a post of the temple of the
> LORD.
> 10 And she was in bitterness of soul, and
> prayed unto the LORD, and wept sore.
> 11 And she vowed a vow, and said, O LORD
> of hosts, if thou wilt indeed look on
> the affliction of thine handmaid, and
> remember me, and not forget thine
> handmaid, but wilt give unto thine
> handmaid a man child, then I will give
> him unto the LORD all the days of his life,
> and there shall no razor come upon his head."
> 1Samuel 1:9-11

> 20 "Wherefore it came to pass, when the time
> was come about after Hannah had conceived,

that she bare a son, and called his name Samuel,
saying, Because I have asked him of the
LORD."
1Samuel 1:20

3.   JACOB WRESTLED all night long, but he pushed
and refused to let go until God blessed him.

26 "And he said, Let me go, for the day
breaketh.
And he said, I will not let thee go, except thou
bless me.
27 And he said unto him, What is thy name?
And he said, Jacob.
28 And he said, Thy name shall be called no
more Jacob, but Israel: for as a prince hast thou
power with God and with men, and hast
prevailed.
29 And Jacob asked him, and said, Tell me, I
pray thee, thy name. And he said, Wherefore is
it that thou dost ask after my name? And he
blessed him there."
Genesis 32:26-29

4.   DANIEL PUSHed even when he knew it would
mean being thrown into the lion's den. He continued to
pray and God sent angels to shut the lion's mouth!

"Then these men assembled, and found Daniel
praying and making supplication before his
God."
Daniel 6:11

"Then the king commanded, and they brought
Daniel, and cast him into the den of lions. Now
the king spake and said unto Daniel, Thy God
whom thou servest continually, he will deliver
thee."
Daniel 6:16

21 "Then said Daniel unto the king, O king, live
for ever.
22 My God hath sent his angel, and hath shut
the
lions' mouths, that they have not hurt me:
forasmuch as before him innocency was found
in me; and also before thee, O king, have I done
no hurt."
Daniel 6:21-22

5.   HEZEKIAH had received a death sentence from God.
But because he PUSHed, God heard his prayer and added
fifteen years to his life!

"Then he turned his face to the wall,
and prayed unto the LORD..."
2 Kings 20:2

5 "...thus saith the LORD... I have heard thy
prayer, I have seen thy tears: behold, I will heal
thee...
6 And I will add unto thy days fifteen years..."
2Kings 20:5-6

Yes, time... after time... after time.... we see how
God honors the persistence of His people... But no
scripture so vividly illustrates the importance of Praying
Until Something Happens like the parable of the widow in
Luke chapter 18. In this passage of scripture we see Jesus
speaking to His followers about the importance of always
praying and not fainting.

In this parable we see a judge who was very evil. He
didn't fear God and he could care less about the welfare of
the people.

All he cared about was himself! In this story there
was also a widow who had been terribly mistreated. The
Bible does not tell us the details surrounding her

misfortune, but we do know that this widow had an adversary. There was someone who didn't like her, there was someone who meant her no good, there was someone who took advantage of her.

People of God, you must understand from the get go, that there will be people who do not like you!

- Everybody's not going to be in your corner...
- Everybody is not going to be excited about how the Lord is blessing you...
- Everybody is not going to be excited about how the Lord has gifted and anointed you....

As long as you live there will be people who hate you, people who SMILE IN YOUR FACE WHILE ALL THE TIME THEY WANNA TAKE YOUR PLACE... BACK STABBERS... BACK STABBERS...

The devil has strategically positioned certain individuals in your life and their sole purpose is to give you grief:

- They may hate you because of the color of your skin...
- They may hate you because of the texture of your hair....
- They may hate you because of the anointing that rests on your life... You may be hated because of the way you walk or talk...
- But rest assured there will be people who just don't like you!!!!

The Bible says that this woman was a widow. Now, I believe that there was significance in this woman being a widow.... You see, a widow is a woman whose husband has died. In Biblical days, women were considered second-class citizens and they were identified by their husbands; so a woman without a husband was hardly even recognized at all. Unless a widow's husband was wealthy and had left her with money, or unless she had sons or other close family members that she could depend on, widows were poor and destitute.

So with that in mind, we can imagine that this widow was a prime target for someone to attack. We can further imagine that this widow would have been among the LEAST likely people that the judge would have helped. But the Bible says that this widow troubled the judge with her persistence! For he said: "Yet because this widow troubleth me, I will avenge her, lest by her continual conming she weary me." In other words, the widow received her request because she wouldn't stop asking. I'm reminded of an old cliché, "The squeaky wheel gets the oil." This widow was a prime example of a "squeaky wheel."

Let's examine the character of this widow…

- She was fully aware of her social status:
- She knew that she was a second class citizen…
- She knew that she didn't have any men to represent her in court…
- She knew that the king was an evil man…
- She knew that she was going to have to take care of her business for herself…
- She knew that there was no one to fight for her…

But in-spite of all of the things that were against her, she had enough confidence in herself and in her God-given rights to keep ON PUSHing!!! She wouldn't take *no* for an answer.

And because of her persistence, this little widow changed public policy, shut the mouths of the nay-sayers and got back everything that the enemy had stolen from her.

You see, sometimes we pray and seek God for things for a while, and when the things that we are praying for don't come as soon as we think they should, we give up. We let doubt and unbelief creep in, and we even sometimes question if we deserve the blessing... Well, I just want to encourage someone today to KEEP *PUSHING*!!!

I can imagine this little old woman approaching the judge day after day, month after month... Each day she would get up in the morning, wash her face, put on her clothes and hike to the king's courts. Regardless of the weather conditions, regardless of the way she was feeling, regardless of what her neighbors were saying about her, she kept pushing! In spite of the king's rejection, she held fast to her conviction and would not stop pursuing the justice that she knew she deserved.

Somebody really needs to get this into your spirit... I feel that somebody has been praying for years and what you've been praying for still hasn't come to pass; but I hear God saying... "DON'T STOP PRAYING."

Understand this: You are going to have to war in the spirit if you are going to get what is rightfully yours. The devil is not just going to let you have your stuff! Satan is a master deceiver! He will trip you up every chance he gets. The enemy's not going to let you see him for what he really looks like; he comes in the form of an illusion. He always presents himself in a wonderful package, but underneath the wrapping is death, hell and the grave!!!

You must understand that what the devil means for evil...

God will turn it around for good!!

1. The very things that the devil sends to take you out...
   a.   God will use those things to build character in you.
2. That pain that you thought you would never heal from...
   a.   God used it to give you greater strength...

   3. When your heart was broken into a thousand
       pieces…
           a. God used that brokenness to draw you
               closer to Him…..
   4. When you were down to your last dime and you
       didn't know how you were going to pay your
       bills…
           a. God used that time in your life to increase
               your faith in Him….

"Yea, and all that will live godly in Christ Jesus
shall suffer persecution."
2Timothy 3:12

So… don't think it strange when the devil hits you
with everything he's got! Just LEARN HOW TO PUSH!!!

Gestation has taken place and that thing that has
been seeded in your belly by the Holy Spirit is ready to be
birthed!!!!! You've been carrying that vision for too long.

You've been carrying that ministry for too
long…You've been carrying that talent for too
long…You've been carrying that anointing for too
long…You've been carrying that healing for too
long…You've been carrying that power for too long…

And now it's time to give birth! Giving birth is not
easy… and it's not fun. Giving birth is painful… Giving
birth is a humbling experience. Even in the natural sense,
when a woman gives birth she is naked, with her legs
wide open. She is in a vulnerable state. Her most private
body parts are exposed. But the woman giving birth
doesn't care about what she looks like at that point, all she
is concerned about is birthing a healthy baby and ending
the pain!

In the spiritual sense, you've got to get naked before
God. You've got to be open and transparent. Regardless
of how you look, regardless of what people may say,

you've got to Face Down and PUSH!!!!! Push past your struggle... Push past your pain... Push past your fears... Push past your bruises... Push past your stronghold... Push past your brokenness... PUSH... PUSH... PUSH!!!

Listen... if you PUSH through adversity... if you PUSH through pain... if you PUSH through your infirmities... if you don't allow the enemy to take you out, your struggles will be the very things that launch you straight into your destiny and purpose!!! Buckle up and Face Down! Don't stop praying!

PUSH - Pray Until Something Happens!

Bibliography

Bowen, Elizabeth. *Mind-Body Medicine: An Overview.*

Golder, Iren Donald. *Tribute - Poetic Lyrics.* Indianapolis.

Kemper KJ, Barnes L. *Medicine, and Spirituality in Pediatrics.*

McCaffrey AM, Eisenberg DM, Legedza AT, et al. *Prayer for Health.*

Perl, Dr. Sheri. *Healing from the Inside Out.*

Roberson, Pastor Dave. *Walk of the Spirit The Walk of Power.*

Stoney, Catherine. *Better Health and Longer Life.* Indianapolis.

The American Heritage Dictionary .

Ward, Bernard. *Think Yourself Well.*

Notes

Notes

Notes